Theologies of American Exceptionalism

RELIGION AND THE HUMAN
Winnifred Fallers Sullivan and Lisa H. Sideris, *editors*

Theologies of American Exceptionalism

Edited by **Winnifred Fallers Sullivan**
and **Elizabeth Shakman Hurd**

INDIANA UNIVERSITY PRESS,
in cooperation with the Center for Religion and the Human, Indiana University

This book is a publication of

Indiana University Press
Office of Scholarly Publishing
Herman B Wells Library 350
1320 East 10th Street
Bloomington, Indiana 47405 USA

iupress.org

© 2021 by The Trustees of Indiana University

Manufactured in the United States of America

First printing 2021

Cataloging information is available from the Library of Congress.

ISBN 978-0-253-06170-6 (hard cover)
ISBN 978-0-253-05656-6 (paperback)
ISBN 978-0-253-05657-3 (ebook)

Contents

V. Chosenness

Preface

Winnifred Fallers Sullivan and
Elizabeth Shakman Hurd

"Thinking Theologically"

In a recent opinion piece on the trial of a white police officer for the murder of an unarmed black man, Botham Jean, J. Kameron Carter revisited Robert Bellah's classic article on civil religion, demanding a reset: "Notwithstanding Bellah's great insight about the operations of American civil religion, what he nonetheless failed to grapple with was the degree to which America as a religious project rooted in the higher ideal or the natural law of human equality and freedom for all rested on an inequality within the ranks of the human ideal of freedom."[1] Like Carter, this volume sees America as a religious project. It is motivated by the notion that what it is to be human is newly under pressure today and nowhere more than in the United States. Joining others who are reinventing theology to address these broader issues, the essayists understand religion to be a question and not an answer.

Invoking the troubling polarization of American life today has become a weary and narcissistic refrain. Notwithstanding these seemingly intractable divisions, however, much important and thoughtful work in various fields is being done to understand and minister to these divisions. Joining this larger conversation, this volume is motivated by the conviction that essential to this effort is making visible the complex and deeply ambivalent religious logics, both explicit and implicit, at work in the various discourses of American exceptionalism. We call this work theological, theology here understood as a broadly inclusive spirit of inquiry, a mode of thought attentive to human finitude. We find with contributor Matthew Scherer that

1. J. Kameron Carter, "How a Courtroom Ritual of Forgiveness Absolves White America." Religion News Service, October 4, 2019, https://religionnews.com/2019/10/04/how-a-courtroom-ritual-of-forgiveness-absolves-white-america/; Robert N. Bellah, "Civil Religion in America," *Dædalus, Journal of the American Academy of Arts and Sciences,* special issue on, "Religion in America" 96, no. 1 (Winter 1967): 1–21. In a footnote to chapter 7 of *Beyond Belief* Bellah clarifies: "I am convinced that every nation and every people come to some form of religious self-understanding whether the critics like it or not" (Oakland, CA: University of California Press, 1970: 168).

vii

much of the resistance to American exceptionalism today is informed by secularist assumptions and preoccupations that "obscure, disavow, or otherwise evade the theological resonances of the exception." Our engagement with this topic thus necessitates, as Joseph Winters reminds us, "a refusal of any solid distinction between the theological and the secular, or religion and politics." Thinking theologically allows us to revisit familiar themes and events with a new perspective; old and new wounds, enduring narratives, and the sacrificial violence at the heart of America are examined while avoiding both the triumphalism of the exceptional and the temptations of the jeremiad. It involves, as Winters recommends, departing from "commitments and investments that have made US exceptionalism so pervasive and commonsensical," and thinking rather with the "unmourned" while remaining "'suspended in the oceanic.'"[2]

We have deliberately sought out spaces not traditionally explored by most theologians. With Cooper Harriss, for example, we turn to novelists as theologians and the "Great American Novel" as theology. Such novels, as Harriss explains, qualify as theological not because they are god-obsessed but rather because of their focus on interiority, the fostering of correspondence between personal and social dimensions of human experience, and the narration of subjectivity within objective frames: "Sounding the distance between internal moral condition and external social order, Great American Novels provide the unbearable evidence of just what such gods require." Lisa Sideris, in her essay, underlines the theological dimensions of American techno-optimism as an antidote to climate disaster, an optimism predicated on Americans' "godlike capacity, our gift for innovation and infinite malleability." Noah Salomon diagnoses "exceptional Americanism" as the moment when the exception seeks to enter into that from which it has been excepted. Circulating through each of these reflections are questions of theology, ultimacy, and the limits of the human.

Theologies of American Exceptionalism is a collection of fifteen interlocking essays reflecting on the vagaries of these and other exceptionalist claims in and about the United States.[3] Loosely and generatively curious,

2. Winters quotes Hortense Spillers: "Mama's Baby, Papa's Maybe: An American Grammar Book," in *Black, White, and in Color: Essays on American Literature and Culture* (Chicago: University of Chicago Press, 2003), 206.

3. As part of the Luce Foundation-supported project "Politics of Religion at Home and Abroad," *Theologies* began to take shape in 2017 when the editors guest-curated a series of paired posts on *The Immanent Frame*, the SSRC's online discussion forum on religion and public life. Two years later these essays seem prescient, noting, as they do, themes and logics

these essays bring together a range of historical and contemporary voices, some familiar and some less so, to stimulate new thought about America.

Contributors were asked to expound on an exemplary text. They chose texts that range from what might usually be regarded as religious texts, such as John Winthrop's "city on a hill" sermon said to have been delivered aboard the *Arabella* and Ruhollah Khomeini's "Last Will and Testament," to judicial opinions, such as that of the US Supreme Court articulating the doctrine of conquest, literary reflections on the Great American Novel, and academic writing on capitalism, consumption, and excess. These texts were not understood to be canonical or exhaustive, but rather suggestive. The essays are presented in pairs under five headings: Love, Fiction, Revolution, Commerce, and Chosen. Five respondents provide further reflection on the paired essays. Read together and in conversation with other reflections on US exceptionalism, the fifteen contributors explore difficult and unresolved aspects of the American project in conversation with the exemplary texts and with each other.

Love. The first two essays, "Familiar Commerce and Covenantal Love" by Constance Furey and "A Yet Unapproachable America" by Matthew Scherer, are followed by a response by Joseph Winters: "The Promise of Immanent Critique." Furey and Scherer stage a conversation between theology and political philosophy, between John Winthrop and Stanley Cavell, highlighting themes of the individual and the community, hierarchy and inequality, tradition and novelty. Each challenges Americans to live up to their exceptionalism. Winters takes exception to their readings by making visible the always outside of the inside created by community, whether triumphal or penitential.

Fiction. The second pair, "A History of America" by Winnifred Fallers Sullivan and "The Great American Novel" by M. Cooper Harriss, are followed by a response from W. Clark Gilpin: "Memories of the Future." Sullivan and Harriss interrogate the theological narratives of two quintessentially secular forms, the Supreme Court opinion and the Great American Novel. In response, Gilpin further explores the tension between fact and fiction in his essay considering the function of national narratives in several classic texts, including the work of Reinhold Niebuhr and Martin Luther King.

---

that have only become more insistent. The initial posts have been expanded and refined for this volume.

Revolution. The third set includes essays by Spencer Dew, "Revolution as Revelation" and Noah Salomon, "Exceptional Americanism" and a response from Faisal Devji: "Unexceptional Islam." Dew the Americanist and Salomon the scholar of Islam undertake a quixotic collaboration, one that began with trading texts, and requiring each to reflect on an unfamiliar text from a tradition he did not specialize in. The result is a remarkable exchange between a scholar of Islam reflecting on a text by Moorish Science founder Noble Drew Ali, and an Americanist writing about Khomeini's "Last Will and Testament." Faisal Devji in response provocatively claims that the Iranian Revolution resulted in a solution to the problem of sovereignty posed by the US Constitution.

Commerce. The fourth set pairs "Techno-Optimism" by Lisa Sideris and "The America-Game" by Elizabeth Shakman Hurd with a response by Elisabeth R. Anker: "Sovereign Exceptionality." Sideris and Hurd carefully expose the productively ambiguous religious languages used to sell "an affective conviction in the United States as transcendent." Sideris displays the remarkable techno-optimism of Americans, uniquely resistant to human responsibility for climate change and endlessly confident that ingenuity will provide a way. Hurd examines Wal-Mart's free enterprise model as an exceptionalist theology that, not unlike Sideris' techno-optimism, naturalizes and depoliticizes a particular understanding of what it means to be American, and to be human. In response Anker reflects on the exceptional investment in sovereign individuality driving both of these stories. Even as sovereign individuality claims universality, she emphasizes, in the United States it is also a subject position available primarily to white men.

Chosenness. Finally, "Sacrifice" by Stephanie Frank and "The Judeo-Christian Tradition" by Shaul Magid are followed by a response by Benjamin L. Berger: "Is the Particular Exceptional?" Frank uses her reading of Paul Kahn as an occasion to reflect on the sacrificial logic inherent in US exceptionalism, the need to constantly manufacture enemies, and to continually seize on the wrong victim, resulting in a form of political idolatry. Magid details the origins and odd journey of "Judaeo-Christian" as a description of America, showing it to be an assimilationist rather than conjunctive gesture, one that enables contemporary forms of Zionist and Americanist politics that specifically exclude the Muslim. Responding from Canada, Berger reflects on the complexity of the universal and the particular in US self-understanding by considering different meanings of the notion of chosenness. It is not merely the fact of particularity but rather the peculiar sacrality of the Constitution that marks US exceptionalism for

Berger. He highlights as a central problematic the need to understand how the particular becomes universal in the American context such that it "has the confidence to traverse other particularities." It is this boundless ethical horizon of American chosenness that aligns with and often seems to precipitate the projection of U.S. military might, markets, and morals around the world.

Together these essays challenge the reader to think America anew.

Acknowledgments

THIS VOLUME WAS DEVELOPED AS A PART OF THE "POLITICS OF RE-
ligion at Home and Abroad" project funded by the Luce Foundation's Initiative on Religion in International Affairs. We gratefully acknowledge
their support, and particularly that of Dr. Toby Volkman who has been a
wonderful colleague to us for many years. We would like to thank Sarah
Dees, Luce Postdoctoral Fellow, for her many contributions to this project, and Matthew Graham and Morgan Barbre for their excellent editorial
assistance in the production of this volume. Thanks to Emily Stratton for
the wonderful cover photo, and to the Department of Political Science and
the Weinberg College of Arts and Sciences at Northwestern University and
the Department of Religious Studies at Indiana University for their support
for this work. Thanks to *The Immanent Frame*, the Social Science Research
Council's online discussion forum on religion and public life, where early
versions of this text appeared. Finally, we are grateful to each of our contributors for taking the time to explore this topic with us.

Note for the Print Edition

THEOLOGIES OF AMERICAN EXCEPTIONALISM WAS PUBLISHED IN 2019 on the Manifold platform, available on the websites of the Center for Religion and the Human at Indiana University and the Indiana University Press: https://publish.iupress.indiana.edu/projects/TAE2019_theologies. Instructors should note that the Manifold edition includes a playlist and permits annotation and other pedagogical engagements with the text that an instructor might want to combine with use of the print edition.

I. Love

1

Familiar Commerce and Covenantal Love

Constance Furey

IN WHAT WAYS IS AMERICAN EXCEPTIONALISM THEOLOGICAL? ON
this point, the significance of John Winthrop's "A Model of Christian Charity" seems obvious.[1] After all, Winthrop's vision of Christian community,
presented to posterity as an address delivered aboard a ship sailing from
England to North America in 1630, concludes by describing the Puritans'
proposed settlement as a "City upon a Hill." This lofty image, memorably
evoked by Ronald Reagan and other twentieth-century politicians, is ri-
valed only by the Statue of Liberty in its ability to represent America's claim
to be set apart from all the other nations of the world, unique in both responsibility and privilege.[2] And unlike the Statue of Liberty, Winthrop's
speech is explicitly biblical and theological. "We must consider that we shall
be as a city upon a hill," Winthrop told his listeners, quoting Matthew 5.14,
and "if we shall deal falsely with our God in this work we have undertaken,
and so cause Him to withdraw His present help from us, we shall be made
a story and a by-word through the world."

Winthrop was not an ordained minister or clergyman, and he had no
advanced training in theology; he was a justice of the peace, elected by the
trustees of the Massachusetts Bay Colony before the erstwhile colonists left
their homeland. He spoke, then, not as a preacher but as a lay Christian
and civic leader, offering a vision of success and failure to people who were
crossing a vast sea in order to—as Winthrop put it—"possess . . . the Good
Land" that awaited them. In the process, historian Sacvan Bercovitch argues, Winthrop created a "formulaic (and unfailingly effective) image of

national purpose." But what exactly is this formula? And why has it been so effective?[3]

Bercovitch's answer to this question is sophisticated and satisfying. It is also—as I will argue in the concluding section of this essay—incomplete. First, Bercovitch explains, in order to understand this formula and its success we need to appreciate the way Winthrop reconciled worldly hierarchy and spiritual unity. In the fallen world, the world Winthrop and his listeners inhabit, there are rich and poor, kings and ministers, the hard realities of commerce and the rightful desire for savings and prosperity. The opening lines of Winthrop's address proclaim that this human inequality is divinely ordained: "God almighty, in His most holy and wise providence, hath so disposed of the condition of mankind, as in all times some must be rich some poor, some high and eminent in power and dignity; others mean and in submission." No one can or should seek to ameliorate differences of rank, or riches, or power.

At the same time—as if in the same breath, Bercovitch says—Winthrop maintains that "all are one" in Christ. The disparate members of the community are "members of one body," "knit together in love." This simultaneous emphasis on unity and hierarchy is a sleight of hand, Bercovitch observes, and especially effective for just this reason. By affirming that God mandates hierarchy, Winthrop upholds the authority of the king who awarded the colony its royal patent and preemptively cautions the artisans, tradesmen, shopkeepers, and independent farmers who made up nearly 80 percent of the Massachusetts Bay Colony company not to think that the profits they sought in the wilderness would turn them all into lords. By insisting that imitating Christ requires loving one another without respect to class or station, Winthrop repurposes a traditional ideal of *imitatio Christi*, transforming what traditionally had been understood as a model of personal piety into a prototype of community. And by admitting no tension between the affirmation of hierarchy and the mandate of unity, Winthrop establishes a model of community well suited to what might otherwise be the conflicting needs of the colonists' new venture.[4]

This model was not royalist: Winthrop says nothing about the divine right of kings and never refers by name to the monarch sitting on the English throne.[5] His immediate concern is not with why kings rule but rather with how communities coalesce. Instead of trying to remind the colonists they are already united as loyal subjects or denizens of Britannia, Winthrop articulates attitudes and ideals that might enable a varied group of people to govern themselves in a new context. In this sense, Winthrop understood that where biblical writers were addressing the Israelites as a people who already self-identified as a tribe, and earlier Christian authors envisioned Christians within the European or Byzantine version of Christendom, his audience was leaving existing models behind. What his predecessors could assume, in other words, Winthrop had to create.[6]

Winthrop's awareness that a shared sense of community was his aim rather than his premise helps explain why a man who believed that hierarchy was divinely ordained would also insist that those on the top of the social pyramid were no better, in the eyes of God, than those on the bottom. Worldly success may be confirmation of the community's adherence to the covenant, but it is not a reflection of individual worth. "It appears plainly," Winthrop says, that "no man is made more honorable than another or more wealthy etc., out of any particular and singular respect to himself." Winthrop's Protestant ethic is communal rather than individual: instead of a Puritan version of the prosperity gospel, Winthrop offers a Puritan version of common purpose. Some are rich and some are poor, but this variation exists so "that every man might have need of others . . . and they might all knit more nearly together."

Winthrop's formula thereby declares that social distinctions are inevitable, even desirable, but also somehow insignificant. In this way, Winthrop sets the terms for America's peculiar disinterest in class differences; his formula both enables and helps to explain the American capacity to tolerate vast and abiding inequalities while feverishly celebrating the ideal of equality and shared purpose.

The second reason Winthrop's image of national purpose was unfailingly effective, according to Bercovitch, is because of the way it melds covenant and contract. Quoting Moses's farewell speech to the Israelites in Deuteronomy 30, Winthrop warns his listeners that their community will flourish in the Promised Land if and only if they follow the commandments. "Beloved," Winthrop intones, "there is now set before us life, and good, and death, and evil in that we are Commanded this day to love the Lord our God, *and to love one another* to walk in his ways and to keep his commandments and his ordinance, and his laws, *and the Articles of our Covenant* with him that we may live and be multiplied, and that the Lord thy God may bless us in the land whither we go to possess it" (Deut. 30.15–16, Geneva Bible, italics mine).

Here Winthrop quotes from the Geneva Bible with slight deviations that highlight key features of his vision. Rather than aligning himself with Moses and speaking in the singular first person, Winthrop counts himself among those being addressed, referring to them all together as a collective "we" (so where the Geneva Bible has "I command thee . . . so that thou mayest live," Winthrop declaims that "we are commanded" so that "we may live"). Where Moses assumed community and focused instead on what this collective needed to do in order to flourish, Winthrop's version makes community itself contingent on their adherence to the commandments: we are "we" only insofar as "we are commanded." Those aboard the ship needed more than a shared destination: Winthrop's vision of common purpose made communal self-definition dependent on fidelity to the covenant.

Equally significant are two clauses Winthrop adds to his biblical source text. Where the Geneva Bible mentions only the commandment to "love the Lord thy God," Winthrop notes also that we are commanded "to love one another." And where Moses is content to list "commandments, ordinances, and laws," Winthrop emphasizes the contractual nature of the relationship by adding "the Articles of our Covenant."[7] The Articles of the Covenant establish the terms of the colonists' venture. If they falter, God's wrath will "break out" against them. The Lord who "ratified this Covenant and sealed our Commission" expected a "strict performance of the Articles contained in it." To succeed, the colonists must "uphold a familiar Commerce together in all meekness, gentleness, patience and liberality." If the community upholds the terms of their agreement, they will prosper. If they abrogate the contract, they will founder. Threatening failure while promising success, Winthrop made communal identity dependent on what Bercovitch aptly describes as this "double 'if.'"

Winthrop's sermon thereby prepared the ground for a notion that came to fruition some seventy years later, when the identity of "Americans" was applied exclusively to white European settlers, especially those settlers commissioned by a Calvinist God. Speaking not as an ordained minister but as the "honorable" and "Esquire" John Winthrop (terms used in the headnote added by his son), the future colonial governor embodied a jurisdictional authority detached from feudal geography and customs.[8] What Winthrop's address rhetorically enables is thus something "broadly modern," Bercovitch concludes, for it associated the promised land in North America not with a nostalgic ideal or existing facts on the ground but with the possibilities of what might be—a contingent community "written into existence by contract and consent," as Bercovitch describes it, "through a declaration of principles and rules that bend religious tradition to legitimate a venture in colonial enterprise."[9] This new world ideal "derives from two traditions that proved inadequate as the framework for modern nationalisms: kingship and Christianity.[10] Winthrop varied both those traditions to accommodate a modern venture, and in the course of variation he opened the prospect for the "America-game."[11]

Novelty thereby becomes a defining feature of the America-game. In fact, Bercovitch contends, Winthrop's sermon was the first "to invest the very concept of newness with spiritual meaning grounded in a specific, then-emergent, now dominant way of life."[12] The philosopher Stanley Cavell is similarly interested in the idea of America as something new under the sun. As Matthew Scherer notes in his essay, Cavell's project is a continuation of the tradition inaugurated by Winthrop's address, transposed from theology to philosophy. Like Winthrop, whom Cavell does not mention, and Ralph Waldo Emerson, his immediate inspiration, Cavell thinks America makes the question of newness inescapable. Like the theologian and philosopher before him, Cavell thinks this newness creates both problems and possibilities and is all the more important for just this reason. America is exceptional, for Cavell as for Winthrop, because of the gap between what is and what could be: neither the theologian nor the philosopher is praising America for being exceptional. Both are instead pointing out the ways—as Scherer aptly explains it—that Americans should take exception to their present shortcomings in order to amend them.

Cavell's philosophy of American exceptionalism also diverges from Winthrop's, however. Where Winthrop applied an old covenant to a new settlement, Cavell associates American novelty with philosophy's capacity to think anew about everyday life and everyday language. Winthrop assumes covenantal exclusivity: the threats of failure and the potential for success apply only to those who are part of the covenantal community. Insofar as the America-game is linked to Winthrop's vision, the difference between the chosen and everyone else is its premise. Cavell refuses that premise, however, when he reimagines American exceptionalism as a philosophical question.

Scherer highlighted this contrast between Cavell's thought and Winthrop's project in oral remarks delivered during the "Theologies of American Exceptionalism" workshop. Carefully delineating twelve figures of exception in Winthrop's text, ranging from Israelites to Christ, from a community figured as a City on a Hill to the commandments of mercy and love, Scherer registered reasons for frustration, even anger, about two points: the fact that nothing shakes Winthrop's presumption of hierarchy, and that all of Winthrop's figures of exception serve to shore up an exclusivist vision of Christian community.

The hierarchy and exclusivity of Winthrop's vision is an important reminder that the America-game is not an innocent project. Moreover, as Cavell's exploratory method attests, philosophy can and should be an antidote to theology's declaration that its claims of truth and certainty reflect the will of an all-powerful and unchanging God. By spiritualizing newness, as Bercovitch says, Winthrop essentially invited subsequent thinkers like Emerson and Cavell to spiritualize their own novel moves: to depart from the tradition he represented, to replace theology with philosophy, and to associate America then not with a new covenant but a new way of thinking.

Insofar as the transition is understood this way, as a shift from authoritarian theology to liberating philosophy, American exceptionalism shifts too. Where theology might declare America a recipient of divine favor—exceptional in its capacity to uphold an ideal and exceptional also in its responsibility to present this ideal as a model for all the other nations of the world—Cavell's version of Emersonian philosophy declares America exceptional in its indeterminacy. We do not know what it means to be new, and so must continually live up to the responsibility of thinking about what this newness entails. This is, I think, an appealing and significant way to think about American exceptionalism.

It is, however, also a way to unthink American exceptionalism, to borrow a term Noah Salomon uses in this forum to describe Noble Drew Ali's approach to American racism.[13] Unthinking exclusionary exceptionalism is a crucial project, and reason enough to call attention to the work of Stanley Cavell as well as Noble Drew Ali. But understanding the appeal of exceptionalism requires us not only to critique its exclusions or unthink its assumptions but also to revisit its canonical sources. This is why Bercovitch's tour de force assessment of Winthrop is invaluable and also why a feature Bercovitch subsumes into his larger argument about unity and diversity needs to be separated out and considered more carefully. Christian charity is Winthrop's stated topic and love his favored theme. Love is the key to both covenant and commerce, in Winthrop's text as in the America-game this text envisions. Put simply, to understand America, we need to understand Winthrop's covenantal theology of love.

* * *

How are we to "uphold a familiar commerce?" Winthrop asks. Here he means commerce in the now nearly obsolete sense of community, but also in the now dominant sense of commercial dealings and the exchange of goods and services. Nearly half of Winthrop's speech is devoted to addressing questions about whether Christians are ever justified in keeping money and goods for themselves, fair rates for lending money, and guidelines for forgiving debts. Editors omit these paragraphs full of fiscal specifics from almost all anthologized versions of Winthrop's famous text,[14] and modern readers might find them easy to skim past, under the assumption that lending rates are only tangentially related to the text's stated topic of "Christian charity," with its connotations of selfless love (from the Latin *caritas*) or philanthropic giving.[15]

In an early section of his talk, Winthrop poses this question: "What rule must we observe in lending?" The answer, he says, requires people to differentiate between those who can repay and those who can't, and so to consider whether the money should be lent "by way of commerce," according to the rule of justice, or by the rule of mercy, for "thou must lend" to one who cannot repay, "though there be danger of losing it." While modern readers may think commerce has little to do with love, these sections reflect a different assumption, for they interweave the languages of love and money as separate threads perceived nevertheless as part of the same tapestry.

Winthrop's text makes visible a series of connections we might otherwise overlook. For Winthrop, "familiar commerce" is synonymous with the communal requirements of the covenant. "Affections of Love" are required to sustain familiar commerce and uphold the articles of the covenant, just as love is the principle that establishes fair and just terms of lending and borrowing money, of borrowing rates and debt forgiveness, and philanthropic giving. "A Model of Christian Charity" thereby makes Christian charity the key to financial success, communal cohesion, and divine approval. This combination of Christianity, commerce, and national purpose remains central to American exceptionalism.

What this argument about the significance of Winthrop's familiar commerce adds to Bercovitch's thesis is, among other things, the claim that Winthrop's formula was unfailingly effective because as theology it was also good psychology. As Winthrop puts it in a succinct defense of his reasons for focusing on love, the "way to draw men to the works of mercy, is not by force of Argument from the goodness or necessity of the work." The argumentative approach may motivate "a rational mind to some present Act of mercy," but claims that a course of action is reasonable or useful "cannot work such a habit in a Soul" as to inspire an eager and willing response. Moreover, love is a requirement of the covenant. By merging attention to covenantal articles with the command to love, Winthrop's lay theology makes everything dependent on relationships—on how the members of the covenantal community feel and act in relation to one another and to God. "We must delight in each other" Winthrop instructs in his most poetic passage. "We must . . . make others' conditions our own; rejoice together, mourn together, labor and suffer together." This sensibility both enables and should be motivated by awareness of "our commission and community in the work, as members of the same body." There is one way, Winthrop says, quoting from the Old Testament, to avoid divine wrath and ensure divine favor: "the only way to avoid this shipwreck, and to provide for our posterity," is to follow the counsel of Micah, to do justly, to love mercy, to walk humbly with our God. What is required is not just to "entertain each other in brotherly affection" but also to share goods and resources: "We must be willing to abridge ourselves of our superfluities, for the supply of others' necessities." This is what upholding a familiar commerce entails, to be "together in all meekness, gentleness, patience and liberality." If these conditions are fulfilled, "the Lord will be our God, and delight to dwell among us, as His own people, and will command a blessing upon us in all our ways, so that we shall see much more of His wisdom, power, goodness and truth, than formerly we have been acquainted with."

We do not often think of the Puritans as sentimental folk, Abram Van Engen recently observed in a study devoted to challenging that assumption.[16] And yet American sentiment cannot be understood without appreciating the Puritan fixation on love and their Calvinist insistence that pious Christians cultivate sympathy and fellow feeling. This Calvinist vision presented sympathy in both active and passive terms, as both as an obligation and something to be discerned and discovered. In Winthrop, we see how this now paradoxical notion of love as a commanded affection, a spontaneous heartfelt feeling that was required to fulfill the terms of the communal compact that was conceived also as a divine contract, came to seem an exceptional feature of American spirituality and then an unremarked aspect of America's self-understanding as a unique and exceptional nation.

The centrality of sentiment is not so easily seen in America's official founding documents, including the Declaration of Independence and the Constitution. Moreover, Winthrop's address disappeared for two hundred years and was not made into an important text until the second half of the twentieth century.[17] Winthrop did not establish the formula, then, in the sense that all subsequent expressions of American exceptionalism cited his text. Winthrop's sermon is a crucial source, rather, because it so powerfully and succinctly encapsulates what it also enables us to see: one crucial reason why Protestantism can, as Winnifred Sullivan has said, shapeshift so easily in America is because this Protestant theology made love an essential feature of American commerce, American culture, American self-understanding and, in short, the American covenant.

Notes

1. John Winthrop, "A Model of Christian Charity," Winthrop Society, accessed February 6, 2018, https://www.winthropsociety.com/doc_charity.php. References to Winthrop's work throughout refer to this source.

2. Ronald Reagan, "We Will Be a City upon a Hill," January 25, 1974, posted on the Federalism and the New Conservatism Website, accessed February 6, 2021, https://patriotpost.us/references/76063-ronald-reagan-we-will-be-a-city-upon-a-hill. An archive of every use of the phrase "city upon a hill" is being developed for the Humanities Digital Workshop at Washington University by Abram Van Engen, last accessed February 6, 2018, https://hdw.artsci.wustl.edu/projects/articles/74?_ga=2.64761839.1701842376.1517925397-850090369.1469651929.

3. Sacvan Bercovitch, "The Winthrop Variation: A Model of American Identity," *Proceedings of the British Academy* 97 (1998): 75–94.

4. For these elements of Bercovitch's argument, see especially 81, and 85–86.

5. Bercovitch, 89n13, 90n14.

6. Bercovitch, 93–94.

7. Winthrop's "Model of Christian Charity" takes citations from both the Geneva Bible and the King James version. On this see Harry Stout, "Word and Order in Colonial New England," in *The Bible in America: Essays in Cultural History,* ed. Nathan O. Hatch and Mark A. Noll (New York: Oxford University Press, 1982), 29 (cited in Brian C. Wilson, "KJV in the USA: The Impact of the King James Bible in the USA," *Comparative Religion Publications,* Paper 2, http://scholarworks.wmich.edu/cgi/viewcontent.cgi?article=1001&context=religion_pubs).

8. Compare to the Virginian natural law founding 150 years later, as described in Winnifred Sullivan's essay in this project, "A History of America."

9. Bercovitch, 91.

10. Bercovitch, 94.

11. The phrase appears on the last page of Bercovitch's essay, but the game motif is his focus throughout. On the America-game, see also Elizabeth Hurd's essay in this volume.

12. Bercovitch, 94.

13. Noah Salomon "Exceptional Americanism," in this project.

14. See, for example, Perry Miller, *The Puritans: Their Prose and Poetry* (Garden City, NY: Doubleday, 1956).

15. Winthrop's essay exposes the contingency of this presumed distinction between finance and spirituality. Numerous recent studies expose the fallacy of this presumption. See, for example, Devin Singh, *Divine Currency: The Theological Power of Money in the West* (Palo Alto: Stanford University Press, 2018) and Kathryn Lofton, *Consuming Religion* (Chicago: University of Chicago Press, 2017). Still to be told, however, is the story of the Protestant roots of this fallacy, especially remarkable given Christianity's long-standing anxiety about usury (memorably analyzed by Lester Little, *Religious Poverty and the Profit Economy* [Utica, NY: Cornell University Press, 1983]) and the evidence of Winthrop's own text, that early modern Protestants were as likely as Catholics and Muslims and others to write about the spiritual significance of monetary dealings.

16. Abram Van Engen, *Sympathetic Puritans: Calvinist Fellow Feeling in Puritan New England* (New York: Oxford University Press, 2015).

17. A story succinctly told by Abram Van Engen in this short video: https://www.youtube.com/watch?v=UISH8k9rcgE, accessed on February 9, 2018.

2

A Yet Unapproachable America

Matthew Scherer

WHERE DO WE FIND OURSELVES? THUS BEGINS RALPH WALDO EMERson's essay "Experience."[1] It's a reasonable place to begin with respect to the problem of "American exceptionalism," and to that of Stanley Cavell's philosophical writings. This short piece follows through on some of Cavell's writings about American exceptionalism in order to highlight a minor tradition that both deserves consideration and stands in constant danger of neglect, forgetting, or perhaps even loss. The ascendance of Trumpism and the profound changes it is installing in American politics—changes that are in some ways reversions, in others novelties—reach to fundamental matters of national identity flying under an exceptionalist banner with the promise to "make America great again." These changes would alone recommend returning attention to the formation of American exceptionalism, including minority, dissenting versions of it. But even beyond its "shithole" president, the United States, I am convinced, is bound in fundamental ways to the problem of the "exception."[2] While this thematic is perhaps indispensable and obvious, Stanley Cavell might seem an unlikely resource to turn to in investigating it. His philosophical voice is only one of many that grapple with American exceptionalism, but the turn he gives to the problem, always subtle, is all the more so now as it has begun to embody the vulnerability of the eclipse that it thematizes. (An important part of Cavell's contribution is an acknowledgment that his is but one possible way of engaging with the question of American exceptionalism, rather than a final or even fully sufficient answer.)

Written about thirty years ago, Cavell's "Finding as Founding,"[3] reads now as a very late but only near-contemporary entry in a relatively long historical tradition of refiguring and reactivating the problem of American exceptionalism. That larger tradition could include John Winthrop's "Model of Christian Charity," reputedly composed and first delivered at sea, between old and new worlds; the first of the *Federalist Papers*, which announces its intention to sway "the fate of an empire in many respects the most interesting in the world"; many of Emerson's essays, including "Experience"; Frederick Douglass's "What to the Slave is the Fourth of July?"; Abraham Lincoln's "Gettysburg Address"; through to James Baldwin's *The Fire Next Time*. That is a rather grand tradition. If Cavell's text can be inserted within it, it also importantly clings within its much more modest local historical circumstances, at the intersection of philosophy and literary theory in the late 1980s. More specifically, Cavell's work emerges at a time in the American academy marked by concern over a growing rift between Francophonic and Anglophonic philosophical traditions and, more specifically still, perhaps somewhere in an anxious, even somewhat defensive, response to the influence of European theory.

That local context clings to it, and as a group at the "Theologies of American Exceptionalism" workshop, we found Cavell's text nearly unreadable, so much that if an answer to the deceptively simple query, *Where do we find ourselves?* with respect to the reception, teaching, and writing of social theory within the academy today seems as little forthcoming as ever, it nonetheless seems clear that we find ourselves somewhere else today than we did thirty years ago. And it seems as little likely today as then that this tradition, such as it is, can be continued. The sustainability of the humanities as a major component of the university, that of the university as a major component within contemporary political economies, that of these same economies within a natural world, are preconditions for social theory as we know it and they are themselves profoundly in question. But I take Cavell's point to be that it has never seemed possible to continue this tradition, perhaps never even possible to begin it.

The very work of traditions, on the other hand, flies in the face of and counters such skepticism about the continuation of a way of life (including Emerson's and Cavell's skepticism about whether we have yet or might ever begin this way of life). Traditions work to set time in joint, to integrate the inchoate within the everyday. Talal Asad, for example, argues that it is a key virtue of traditions to orient the present toward the future with respect to its past by giving shape to a form of life at those points where language and bodies are bound within the "minutiae of everyday living." Asad sets that argument against the thoroughgoing problematization of the very possibility of a *modern* tradition powerfully thematized by thinkers such as Hannah Arendt and Alasdair MacIntye.[4]

We began our conversation by pairing two texts, what has become the unavoidable urtext, Winthrop's conjuration of a city on a hill, with an artifact of Cavell's career, a minor text indeed. And so we found ourselves, a group of scholars who could not quite bring themselves to read with confidence and conviction a thirty year old work of philosophy, reading it, and reading it without an open suspicion that it may be "fraudulent" in the sense of being a remnant of a passing fad, or a mere reiteration of a thought had many times before and after. And this minor circumstance mirrors, I think, a point that can be drawn from Cavell's text: if the major forms of the American exception, the "Cities on the Hill," are an overwhelming presence, the alternatives to it are obscure, frustrating, and doubtful. Insofar as Cavell recommends attention to a variety of minor, everyday, ordinary exceptions, our capacities to respond to these narrow contexts—wrapped in something as arcane, dismal even, as the mid-century rise of logical positivism in American departments of philosophy (responding to which as a student, Cavell writes, "became as if on the spot an essential part of my investment in what I would call philosophy")—may be what matters most.[5]

Obscurity, frustration, doubt—precisely when we might no longer care terribly much about the particular points disputed, or more pointedly, precisely where we think what was in dispute did not matter, where we think there was nothing exceptional to begin with, Emerson's and Cavell's question of how one might begin to work within a tradition to produce new kinds of exceptions appears. That fact is meant to be disconcerting, for as Cavell observed in one of his earliest publications, "the dangers of fraudulence, and of trust, are essential to the experience of art. If anything in this paper should count as a thesis, that is my thesis. And it is meant quite generally. Contemporary music is only the clearest case of something common to modernism as a whole, and modernism only makes explicit and bare what has always been true of art."[6] The emphasis here might be placed on *trust*. I take it to be—in part—that those things that matter (exceptions, artworks, ideas) are always a bit suspect, elusive, vulnerable to fraudulence, and requiring trust in another world of relationships—the trust that would sustain them.

We will loop back to the relatively fine point I am trying to make here, but it is important also to note that much of what Cavell has to say can also be put plainly, and in this he pursues a line of thought easily discernible in Winthrop, Publius, Emerson, Douglass, Lincoln, and Baldwin. Here it is not that Americans are an exceptionally blessed, virtuous, or accomplished people. Much to the contrary, the point is that the American people must be spurred to transcend their all-too-compromised circumstances. In its basic outlines, the idea is that the people at large must be converted to a new set of values, a new way of life, a new world. The idea is not to praise Americans as an exceptional people, but rather to press Americans to take exception to their present shortcomings in order to begin amending them. As Emerson's "Experience" puts it, echoing a theology of conversion, the thought is that "I am ready to die out of nature and be born again into this new yet unapproachable America I have found in the West."

If Emerson is often interpreted as an American triumphalist, much of Cavell's thrust in reading Emerson is to inoculate American exceptionalism against that impulse by insisting on the tragic dimension of America's unapproachability. Cavell suggests an exceptionalism in which the leading notes are those of determined criticism, rather than celebration; aspirational solidarity rather than historical or ethnic nationalism; dissent and resistance rather than a self-sacrificing love of country. The exhortation is addressed to Americans not because they are an especially worthy people, but rather because when we ask, "Where do we find ourselves?" the answer is that we find ourselves in America, among a people who might yet become Americans. This remains an exceptionalism, but it is a severely chastened one such that enacting the American exception is bound up with acknowledging the failure (as yet) to attain America's promise. Despite the apparent dominance of chauvinistic white nationalisms in the history of American exceptionalisms, Cavell would remind us, there might be a minor though no less American tradition that takes exception to those dominant forms.

This tradition maintains that ethical, political, and spiritual life depend upon cultivating people's willingness to take exception to their way of life in the name of something better. Taking exception, however, requires a way of thinking, a kind of practice that has to be continually renewed and reinvented; thus, it involves a tradition rather than a definitive statement, concept, or origin. To enact American exceptionalism in this sense is to find a new answer to the question, "How does one conceive (think and enact) America's novelty, and this as an inheritance and transfiguration of a distinct spiritual tradition?" Taking this question from Cavell, rather than Emerson or Winthrop, suggests a bit more clearly that it may yet be a living question, rather than a merely historical artifact. Taking this quite recent form might let us wonder how much resistance to all claims of

American exceptionalism are formed by a near-contemporary secularism that obscures, disavows, or otherwise evades the theological resonances of the exception. It may also let us wonder a bit about our contemporary post-secularist context that solicits reconsideration of those resonances.

Cavell suggests that for an American philosopher, serious thinking must pass through the question of how to create an exception, that is to say that to think seriously is to discover how to think creatively within one's own tradition. To put that another way, Cavell insists upon producing an American exception—in his particular professional and intellectual context, that meant finding in Emerson's response to Kant the path for serious/philosophical thought after Heidegger and Wittgenstein. That Cavell puts this as a question for philosophy, however, seems a consequence of his own professional formation, or perhaps his effort to find his own voice in turning away from this formation. While Cavell's focus falls on creating an exception within his own field of philosophy, it stands to reason that serious work in a number of fields—literature, the arts, theology, political theory, politics—might also pass through this same question. Throughout his writing Cavell insists upon the idea that a certain kind of thinking, questioning, criticizing, and writing becomes qualitatively different, in a word, "serious." In Cavell's words, there is "an obligation of any writer who takes on, perhaps beyond her or his will, certain, let's call them scriptural tasks" that include "struggling to keep its moral urgency" through establishing "the right to philosophize, to reconceive reason."[7] That right must constantly be re-established—it is exceptional.

While this seems to me to be one way of following out Cavell's thought, and well enough on its own, it both fails to find the bottom of it, and also fails to locate its difference from the underlying refrain established in, for example, Winthrop's "Model of Christian Charity," as it is so lucidly articulated by Constance Furey in chapter 1 of this volume. Furey, extending Sacvan Bercovitch's analysis, exposes the intermediate texture of human relations opened as it were beneath the canopy of Winthrop's model of charity. The movement of Winthrop's text, and the "America-game" that it inaugurates, is shown, in Furey's rendering, as triumphal only insofar as it draws an open compass within which indeterminate, ever-to-be-renewed human agents are to enact an overarching but abstract injunction to love within *the minutiae of everyday life*. Furey renders this as a space of careful discernment, self-interrogation, change, and redirection. She also reminds us that in America, from Winthrop's time to our own, everyday life has been *commercial life*. If Cavell draws modern philosophy toward theology by way of mutual commitment to conversion,[8] Furey seems to meet him there in drawing theology toward philosophical modernism through this range of concerns.

What then does Cavell add to the game of American exceptionalism if Winthrop himself had already embodied both dogmatic certainty and high modernist discernment amid uncertainty, both scripturally grounded Pauline love and attention to the nuances of affectively imbued social relations? Cavell has reminded us that democracy requires "preparation to withstand not its rigors but its failures, character to keep the democratic hope alive in the face of disappointment with it."[9] But, however satisfying that idea may be, it has been cited many times already, and moreover, Cavell offers it openly at second hand, from Emerson's mouth, and thus surely not as an innovation. Indeed, "Finding as Founding," is an extended meditation on Emerson—why, if the claim is on behalf of innovation, of finding one's own voice, is it lodged within—ventriloquized through—the voice of another? What if there is nothing of Cavell's here—vis-a-vis Emerson, or vis-a-vis Winthrop—in which case the text would be "fraudulent" in the sense of passing another's thoughts, insights, inventions, off as one's own?

One of the most consistent effects of Cavell's work is to cause the floor to drop out from under his readers. He causes us to entertain the notion that we are suspended over an abyss, not unlike Jonathan Edwards's sinners in the hand of an angry God, inviting (more, requiring) us to confront the possibility of fraud, the possibility that this text is broken, that it makes no new link in a tradition, that there was no tradition there worth linking to. A shithole text. That's all that some readers, sometimes, can see, myself included—shithole readers. This is an experience that, in Cavell, as much as in Edwards, is both unsustainable and indispensible. It is something to pass through, to pass on from hopefully, rather than to avoid or disavow. "What happens to philosophy if its claim to provide foundations is removed from it—say the founding of morality in reason or in passion, of society in a contract, of science in transcendental logic, of ideas in impressions, of language in universals or in a formalism of rules?" Cavell asks. But he continues:

> Finding ourselves on a certain step we may feel the loss of foundation to be traumatic, to mean the ground of the world falling away, the bottom of things dropping out, ourselves foundered, sunk on a stair. But on another step we may feel this idea of (lack of) foundation to be impertinent, an old thought for an old world. (The idea of foundation as getting to the bottom once and for all of all things is a picture Thoreau jokes about in describing, in "The Pond in Winter" and "Conclusion" in *Walden*, the time he took measurements of the bottom of Walden, and times such measurements become controversial.) The

step I am taking here is to receive the work of "Experience" as transforming or replacing founding with finding and to ask what our lives would look like if the work is realized.[10]

This attitude of finding humor where we founder, of making jokes at our loss of connection with tradition, is worth sitting with for a moment at America's present impasse. Taking more steps here in this tradition rather than remaining sunk on our stair calls for a great deal of trust, trust precisely unfounded in our tradition. This is something to contemplate closely when today's dominant form of American exceptionalism is so tightly wrapped in racism, xenophobia, sexism, outright brutality toward the most vulnerable, callous disregard for the future, unbound commerce, and waning democracy—so tightly wrapped that we might well wonder if there had ever been a different tradition than this.

This settling with absence, impossibility, and failure may be one of the points at which Cavell's exceptionalism pulls Winthrop hardest in a new direction. Cavell's treatment of Winthrop's central theme, "Love," shines some light on this. On what seems the most direct reading, Winthrop enjoins his listeners to love, demands it of them. If there is a thesis to "A Model of Christian Charity," this would be it:

> By the first of these lawes man as he was enabled soe withall is commanded to love his neighbour as himself. Upon this ground stands all the precepts of the morrall lawe, which concernes our dealings with men, . . . [and] therefore the exhortation must be generall and perpetuall, withallwayes in respect of the love and affection, . . . [and] soe this definition is right. Love is the bond of perfection . . . [and] for to love and live beloved is the soule's paradise both here and in heaven . . . [and] now the onely way to avoyde this shipwracke, and to provide for our posterity, is to followe the counsell of Micah, to doe justly, to love mercy, to walk humbly with our God.[11]

These exhortations might be compared with the aging king's solicitation of love at the opening of Shakespeare's *King Lear* and with Cavell's interpretation of *Lear* in "The Avoidance of Love," which turns to a great extent on this opening scene, and on the conjoined solicitation and avoidance that his title invokes (running to roughly eighty pages, it addresses many other things besides). Abdicating his throne, King Lear offers to divide what is his and pledge it to his daughters in return for a public profession of their love:

> Tell me, my daughters,
> Since now we will divest us both of rule,
> Interest of territory, cares of state,
> Which of you shall we say doth love us most?
> That we our largest bounty may extend."

This promise of "our largest bounty" in return for the greatest public performance of love, clearly recalls the terms of Winthrop's "double-if." "This is the way I understand that opening scene with the three daughters," Cavell writes,

> Lear knows it is a bribe he offers, and—part of him anyway—wants exactly what a bribe can buy: (1) false love; and (2) a public expression of love. That is: he wants something he does not have to return in kind, something which a division of his property fully pays for. And he wants to look like a loved man—for the sake of the subjects, as it were. He is perfectly happy with his little plan, until Cordelia speaks. Happy not because he is blind, but because he is getting what he wants, his plan is working. Cordelia is alarming precisely because he knows she is offering the real thing, offering something a more opulent third of his kingdom cannot, must not, repay; putting a claim upon him he cannot face. She threatens to expose both his plan for false love with no love, and expose the necessity for that plan—his terror of being loved, of needing love.[12]

While I can't promise to get to the bottom of scripture, Shakespeare, or Cavell on the question of love, I think we can find a difference between Cavell and Winthrop here, or a difference Cavell's reading would introduce to Winthrop's text. Where the one enjoins love, the other asks us to consider why we are tempted to demand love, what we avoid in the demand, and how the appearance of "the real thing" often takes the tragic form of spoiling our plans, or more precisely, revealing our plans to have been rotten from the start. Beneath the fraudulent surface, something more real hides in obscurity, frustration, and doubt.

One of the key questions Cavell poses is how a thinker can create exceptions within the ordinary fabric of the everyday world and of everyday language. While Cavell hastens to translate these concerns into a "philosophical" register, they clearly draw upon and resonate with key theological motifs and religious practices. They reach beyond the confines of professional philosophy. Cavell acknowledges that the production of the exception is a key question in Biblical traditions—in Deuteronomy, for example, and also in the New Testament—and within the traditions of spiritual practice articulated with those texts, including but not limited to conversion. While we won't tarry with the possible implications of that, neither Cavell nor I are committed to separating "religion" or "theology" or "philosophy" from other forms of life. I would say in conclusion that if the idea of America is indeed bound to that of the exception, that does not mean that this idea can be reduced to the current push to "restore American greatness." Nor does it mean that it can be reduced to its best prior historical exemplars. In answer to Emerson's query, this might all suggest that we find ourselves very much still engaged with the question of the American exception, not only because virulent waves of American exceptionalism are coursing through our politics in a variety of forms—they seem always to have done so—but also because rethinking the exception is how we go about continuing the tradition we find ourselves within, even when that might seem hopeless.

Vanity, greed, ambition, ignorance, arrogance, aggression, bankruptcy, white-supremacy, misogyny, bluster, and lies, lies, lies—in promising to "Make America Great Again," America's "shithole" presidency might ironically accomplish the task of focusing national attention on the ways that America's historical failures continue within its present, and on the constant need to return to and remain with those failures with honesty and a commitment to address and redress them, rather than to continue a triumphant tradition that disavows and otherwise avoids them. Today's exceptionalism, arguably *through its triumphalist disavowals*, solicits these minor chords with intense urgency. "What seems to me evident is that Emerson's finding of founding as finding, say the transfiguration of philosophical grounding as lasting, could not have presented itself as a stable philosophical proposal before the configuration of philosophy established by the work of the later Heidegger and the later Wittgenstein," Cavell notes in a striking aside.[13] It is perhaps in the same way that it has only recently become possible to find critical resources within Winthrop's sermon. And this is another reason to imagine that we have not yet found the bottom of the tradition of American exceptionalism. And that we might yet find a way to go on with it.

Notes

1. Ralph Waldo Emerson, "Experience," Emerson Central, accessed February 23, 2021, https://emersoncentral.com/texts/essays-second-series/experience/. Originally published in *Essays: Second Series* (Boston: J. Munroe, 1844); quotes refer to the online edition.

2. As reported in the *New York Times* on January 11, 2018, and widely covered elsewhere, "President Trump on Thursday balked at an immigration deal that would include protections for people from Haiti and some nations in Africa, demanding to know at a White House meeting why he should accept immigrants from 'shithole countries' rather than from places like Norway, according to people with direct knowledge of the conversation." "Trump Alarms Lawmakers with Disparaging Words for Haiti and Africa," *New York Times*, January 11, 2018, https://www.nytimes.com/2018/01/11/us/politics/trump-shithole-countries.html.

3. Stanley Cavell, "Finding as Founding," chap. 6 in *Emerson's Transcendental Etudes* (Stanford, CA: Stanford University Press, 2003).

4. See Talal Asad, "Thinking About Tradition, Religion, and Politics in Egypt Today," *Critical Inquiry*, Features, accessed February 22, 2021, https://criticalinquiry.uchicago.edu/thinking_about_tradition_religion_and_politics_in_egypt_today/; Hannah Arendt, "Tradition and the Modern Age," chap. 1 in *Between Past and Future* (New York: Viking, 1961); and Alasdair MacIntyre, *Three Rival Versions of Moral Enquiry: Encyclopaedia, Genealogy, and Tradition* (London: Gerald Duckworth, 1990).

5. Stanley Cavell, *Little Did I Know: Excerpts from Memory* (Stanford, CA: Stanford University Press, 2010), 253.

6. Stanley Cavell, "Music Discomposed," chap. 7 in *Must We Mean What We Say?*, updated ed. (Cambridge: Cambridge University Press, 2015), 175.

7. Stanley Cavell, introduction to *Emerson's Transcendental Etudes* (Stanford, CA: Stanford University Press, 2003), 6–7.

8. In his interpretation of Thoreau's *Walden*, which emphasizes the problems of "economy," Cavell makes clear too that what is at stake in the American framework is a recovery of the spiritual within the context, through the conversion of, commercial life.

9. Stanley Cavell, "Aversive Thinking," chap. 1 in *Conditions Handsome and Unhandsome* (Chicago: University of Chicago Press, 1990), 56.

10. Stanley Cavell, "Finding as Founding," 134.

11. John Winthrop, "A Model of Christian Charity" (Boston: Collections of the Massachusetts Historical Society, 1630), available online through Hanover Historical Texts Collection, https://history.hanover.edu/texts/winthmod.html.

12. Stanley Cavell, "The Avoidance of Love," chap. 10 in *Must We Mean What We Say?*, 266–67.

13. Stanley Cavell, "Finding as Founding," 139.

3

The Promise of Immanent Critique

Joseph Winters

US EXCEPTIONALISM IS A DISCIPLINARY MECHANISM THAT SIMUL-
taneously reproduces the idea of America's singularity and the burden of
bearing universal values and principles.[1] The "American difference" implies
a kind of transcendence or separation with regard to other nation-states
and populations; at the same time America's others are supposed to emulate
the United States as the global standard, measure, and telos of democracy,
freedom, and human flourishing. As an exception, the United States establishes and embodies the law while giving itself the authority to act outside
the law, to turn its exception into a kind of hidden rule.[2] Following Agamben, we might say that this ability to act within and without, inside and
outside, the legal order is a special case of sovereignty, a notion that over-
flows any rigid theological-secular binary. Consequently, if the nation-state
is a secular entity, then the secular is often a re-articulation of (Christian)
theological commitments. And as a disciplinary framework, this logic of
the sovereign exception shapes and organizes the body politic; it is a constitutive part of the formation of American political subjectivity. This was
demonstrated in late 2014 when people criticized the Obama administration for creating new relationships with Cuba—with a regime that has violated human rights—at the same that a major report was released detailing
the United States' longstanding practice of torture and other human rights
violations. While this might seem ironic, the semantics of exceptionalism
renders these two realities consistent. America can act outside the law because we do this in the name of health, life, and order. Departing from
global rules is acceptable when this transgression is done for the sake of

populations that are more valuable, more worthy of life, and closer to what we might call the sacred.

Sacvan Bercovitch reminds us that this logic of the exception is insidious; it is not always explicit, and it is not always attached to conservative political projects.[3] In fact, Bercovitch contends that exceptionalism has provided a common ground or consensus among conservatives and progressives, Ronald Reagan and Martin Luther King Jr. For a progressive like King—following in the footsteps of Emerson—the critique of American corruption is emboldened by a commitment to the notion that America has a special responsibility to the rest of the world. The rejection of racism, greed, or empire is inspired by a gap between the ideal of America and its current reality. This gap is the result of Americans not living up to the promise of democracy, to their special onus, a burden that is both singular and universalizing. For a more recent example of a progressive use of this logic, we might think of Colin Kaepernick's valiant, and costly, attempt to mourn Black death during the national anthem ritual before NFL games. When questioned about his decision to kneel and refrain from reciting the anthem, he replied: "This country stands for liberty, justice, for everyone. And it's not happening for all right now. . . . I have family, I have friends that have fought for this country. They fight for liberty and justice, for everyone. . . . I mean, people are dying in vain because this country is not holding its end of the bargain up as far as giving freedom and justice and liberty to everybody."[4] While Kaepernick's protest is directed toward the failure to live up to certain lofty, democratic notions, the sacred quality of these notions (liberty, justice for all) is not questioned; in addition the close linkage between America and freedom, not to mention America's capacity to strive and fight for "everyone," is left unchallenged. The problem, Kaepernick suggests, is that the country is not "holding up its end of the bargain," not living up to its professed ideals, especially when it comes to Black people and military veterans. One can imagine another kind of interpretation that would question the intrinsic purity of these ideals, that would show how "our" freedom and justice, rather than being fought for everyone, is always intertwined with coercion, suffering, dispossession, and danger for some community.

Kaepernick's jeremiad prompts us to ask a series of related questions: Can we simply abandon the idea of the American exception or must we work through its ambivalent legacies? Is a progressive critique of America always bound up with the proverbial idea of America, the genius and promise of America, and so forth? If not, are there traditions that offer us something different even as they get obscured by the very language of tradition? Is US exceptionalism unique or a subset of nation-state sovereignty and its paradoxical relationship to the law? Can we understand the pernicious implications of US singularity apart from a cluster of related conditions and arrangements—settlement, property, racism, war, and empire? How does an engagement with US exceptionalism necessitate a refusal of any solid distinction between the theological and the secular, or religion and politics?

The contributors to *Theologies of American Exceptionalism* offer powerful responses to these kinds of questions. In particular, Constance Furey and Matthew Scherer demonstrate what an immanent critique of American exceptionalism looks like. As I take it, Furey and Scherer acknowledge the violent kernel of the grammar of American singularity but insist that we can read this framework against itself. In other words, we might return to key authors and texts within the tradition of American thought with the aim of discovering tensions, gaps, and unexplored possibilities. While Furey directs us to John Winthrop's well-known "City Upon a Hill" sermon, Scherer examines Stanley Cavell's essay "Finding as Founding." By juxtaposing Winthrop and Cavell, the reader might expect Furey and Scherer to underscore the distinction between theology and philosophy, between the affirmation and rejection of America's divine election. But the authors refuse this simple contrast. As they point out, "Cavell's philosophy both inherits and transfigures Winthrop's theological tradition, suggesting the capacity of traditions, including theological traditions for fluidity, novelty, and diversity."[5] In what follows, I want to think through this Winthrop-Cavell pairing, the promise of immanent critique, and the im/possibility of imagining an outside, or otherwise, to the American exception.

Furey's insightful reading of Winthrop's 1630 sermon "A Model of Christian Charity" is inspired by the possibility that we might read this text anew. With a kind of careful discernment, the reader might ferret out a more critical set of possibilities in Winthrop's sermon. Furey urges and performs a patient, nuanced reading of this early source of America's collective self-image. She begins by invoking Bercovitch's claim that Winthrop "reconciled worldly hierarchy and spiritual unity."[6] Even as his sermon endorses the kinds of divisions (rich and poor, kings and ministers) that exist in a fallen world, it also underscores the "all brothers in Christ" motif. In fact, we might say that the hierarchical, demonstrated by the covenantal relationship between God and human, depends on the horizontal and contractual relationships between members of a community. Or to put it differently, fulfilling the covenant obligates the members of the Puritan community to treat each other with respect, love, patience, and humility. And what is important for Furey is that Winthrop does not necessarily presuppose a coherent community; his community is contingent upon obeying God's commandments on new land, in a New Jerusalem. Winthrop's "shared sense of community was his aim rather than his premise"[7]; and this coming community does not allow hierarchical relationships to prevent intimacy between the highest and the lowest. More generally, an emphasis on a community to come, rather than a community already established, makes room for indeterminacy, novelty, and contingency.

What intrigues Furey about Winthrop's sermon is his "covenantal theology of love." For Winthrop, love and commerce are intertwined. A love ethic, he exhorts, should regulate lending and borrowing practices, debt forgiveness, and philanthropic activities. As Furey puts it, "By merging attention to covenantal articles with the command to love, Winthrop's lay theology makes everything dependent on relationships—on how the members of the covenantal community feel and act in relation to one another and to God."[8] Consequently, Winthrop's vision of being together includes a salient affective component; it involves collective delight, mourning, suffering, and exaltation. And perhaps it is here that we should introduce some questions about the language of love, affect, community, and body that make up Winthrop's covenantal theology. For instance, what is the relationship between love and hatred, or delight and repulsion? Intense feelings of love and intimacy within a community often involve the displacement of antipathy and rancor toward internal and external others. Similarly, the very formation of community relies on the fabrication of an outside, a threatening exterior that the community defines itself over and against. Dependence and violence are not incompatible. Another way to say this is that the kinds of relationships that Winthrop's God commands (relationships that involve varying degrees of amiability and hostility) are enabled by a tacit contrast with a set of *antagonistic non-relationships.* By antagonism, I am alluding to positions and populations that constitute an exception to the rule of love and charity, those who can be systemically killed or displaced without much moral outrage.[9]

Yet how we assess Winthrop's theological response to these matters depends on how we read various passages in his City on the Hill sermon. For instance, when Winthrop enjoins his audience to "love the enemy" (in line with Matthew 5:44), we might wonder who the "enemy" includes. Even though the term "enemy" acknowledges an antagonistic other that the

Christian is obligated to love, the enemy is still an-other that is recognized and included within the Puritan's ethical sphere. What we have to consider are those others, or populations below the level of alterity, that the jeremiad necessarily assimilates and erases, or always already relegates to the status of nothingness. More specifically, we have to think through the indigenous communities, practices, and ways of relating to the earth that are obscured by the language of "that the Lord our God may *bless us* in the *land* whither we go to *possess* it."[10] The divine right to possession, combined with the ways in which Winthrop sanctifies posterity and future prosperity, is insidious. This early grammar of exceptionalism both relies on and disavows the intimacy between life and death, expansion and erasure, possession and theft, property and violence, the imagination of newness and the conversion of what already exists (but that gets in the way of a new enterprise) to non-being.

What I am trying to get at are the structural constraints to any re-reading of Winthrop's sermon and the jeremiad tradition. Furey brilliantly redirects our attention to the covenantal grammar of love and relationality in "A Model of Christian Charity," grammar that provides resources for internal critique and revision. At the same time, the very logic of community or the collective body that Winthrop works with—and that we inherit—puts severe constraints on our ability to reimagine love, intimacy, and being with recalcitrant others. Perhaps one way to push Winthrop on these matters is to think through the distinction between body and flesh, terms that are used throughout his sermon. Focusing more on the notion of a unified collective body, Winthrop writes:

> There is no body but consists of parts and that which knits these parts together, gives the body its perfection, because it makes each part so contiguous to others as thereby they do mutually participate in with each other, both in strength and infirmity, in pleasure and pain. . . . The several parts of this body considered a part before they were united, were as disproportionate and as much disordering as so many contrary qualities and elements, but when Christ comes, and by his spirit and love knits all these parts to himself and each to other, it is become the most perfect [without spot or wrinkle] and best proportioned body in the world (Ephesians 4: 15–16).[11]

Here the body is associated with unity, perfection or perfectibility, proportion, and order. The collective Christian body is implicitly defined in contrast to disorder, scattering, discordance, impurity, and wildness. This implies that the Puritan communal body is fabricated and formed in opposition to populations and communities that have been made to signify wildness and impurity. Hortense Spillers, an author who is thinking about another voyage across the sea, writes: "But I would make a distinction . . . between the 'body' and 'flesh' and impose that distinction as the central one between captive and liberated subject-positions. In that sense, before the 'body' there is the 'flesh,' that zero degree of social conceptualization that does not escape concealment under the brush of discourse or the reflexes of iconography."[12] Flesh for Spillers indicates both the severability of captive bodies and an excess that escapes the general thrust toward transparency. An ethics of the flesh, which certainly bears a connection to Christianity, involves an intimacy with those beings, entities, desires, and energies that interrupt yearnings for coherence, settlement, and so on. It entails a difficult, and wounded, vulnerability to that which is opaque, indeterminate, and exorbitant. This is in no way incompatible with love but decouples love from Winthrop's unified sense of the corporate body.

As Scherer contends, the legacy of the exception, especially as it gets transformed by Emerson and Cavell, might be compatible with this wounded ethics. For Scherer, Cavell's essay "Finding as Founding" represents a minor key within the American tradition and a reminder that the United States is "bound in fundamental ways to the problem of the 'exception.'"[13] In this essay by Cavell, Scherer finds an alternative notion of the American exception. He writes: "Here it is not that Americans are an exceptionally blessed, virtuous, or accomplished people. Much to the contrary, the point is that the American people must be spurred to transcend their all-too-compromised circumstances."[14] To take exception is not only to be offended by the ways in which American exceptionalism is "so tightly wrapped in racism, xenophobia, sexism, and outright brutality toward the most vulnerable."[15] This disposition also suggests that "people must be converted to a new set of values, a new way of life, a new world."[16] Taking exception, in other words, exists at the intersection of critique and hope, and rejection and creation. For Cavell, the issue for Americans is not so much defending our exceptional status in the world; the real burden is to "create an exception,"[17] to produce novel ideas and possibilities, an activity that is enabled by serious thought and reflection.

According to Scherer, Cavell puts a twist on the exceptionalist tradition by playing with the language of "finding and founding." For Cavell, we occasionally "find" ourselves looking at and over an abyss, a reminder that our practices, thoughts, and projects lack any solid foundation. This recognition of the abyss may initially be a source of trauma and despair, but Cavell encourages us, as Scherer puts it, to find "humor where we *founder*."

And to settle with, and be unsettled by, "absence, impossibility, and failure" requires trust, vulnerability, and forms of sociality that do not yet exist. Perhaps at this point we should introduce and consider some questions and tensions regarding Cavell's rethinking of the exception and national foundation. What possibilities open up when we think about the idea of America alongside the abyss, the bottom? Riffing on the title of Scherer's essay, "A Yet Unapproachable America," we might ask what it means to juxtapose the nation with waste, excess, dirt, and abjection.[18] While the position of the sovereign nation-state both exceeds and protects the order of things, "shit" and dirt also represent that which cannot be assimilated into the social order, or that which has to be spurned for the sake of order. In fact, we might say that the nation-state and its promise of recognition is supposed to protect the recognized from being identified with formlessness, disorder, and death. Would an unapproachable America, an America imagined in terms of dirt and waste, be a recognizable community? Or would this conjunction of nationhood and filth point toward ways of being together that exceed the nation-state and the related logics of sovereignty, triumph, and settlement?

Among other important provocations, Scherer extends Furey's insistence on immanent critique. On his reading, we are "bound . . . to the problem of the 'exception'" and the traditions that have inherited, passed down, and rearticulated this problem. According to Scherer, "we find ourselves very much still engaged with the question of the American exception, not only because virulent waves of American exceptionalism are coursing through our politics . . . but also because rethinking the exception is how we go about continuing the tradition we find ourselves within."[19] As this passage suggests, we cannot simply discard US exceptionalism; it continues to shape and haunt political life and any critique of the American exception finds itself within a set of discourses that we reanimate even as we refuse and denounce them. But there is always a subtle relationship between a within and a without, the inside and the outside. In other words, by identifying the tensions, fissures, and possibilities within the tradition of the exception, one also points to an exterior, an excess, that cannot be captured by the grammar of US exceptionalism.

One way to connect the immanent to this outside is by returning to the location of Winthrop's sermon—the sea, in between two worlds, the unstable waters. (Remember that Winthrop imagines the City on the Hill as the alternative to a shipwrecked condition.) By highlighting the in-between space of the sea, the turbulent flow of dark water, two alternative lines of flight come into view. For one, the land of America is decentered while the flows, connections, and violent intimacies among continents emerge into the foreground.[20] More specifically, the sea conjures up another history of voyages and relocations that occurred alongside the Puritan search for a new home. Dark water reminds us of the kidnapped African bodies at the *bottom* of the ocean; those unmourned bodies that can never be completely folded into a national project or a redemptive sense of posterity. To think with the unmourned, to be "suspended in the oceanic,"[21] is one way to depart from commitments and investments that have made US exceptionalism so pervasive and commonsensical.

Notes

1. See Jasbir Puar, *Terrorist Assemblages: Homonationalism in Queer Times* (Durham, NC: Duke University Press, 2007), 8.

2. Here I am indebted to Agamben's reflections on sovereignty in *Homo Sacer: Sovereign Power and Bare Life*, trans. Daniel Heller-Roazen (Stanford: Stanford University Press, 1998), 15.

3. See Bercovitch, *The American Jeremiad* (Madison: University of Wisconsin Press, 1978), 176–210.

4. Colin Kaepernick, "Transcript: Colin Kaepernick Addresses Sitting during National Anthem," *USA Today*, NinersWire, transcript by Chris Biderman, August 28, 2016, https://ninerswire.usatoday.com/2016/08/28/transcript-colin-kaepernick-addresses-sitting-during-national-anthem/.

5. Quoted from Furey and Scherer's correspondence regarding this work.

6. Constance Furey, "Familiar Commerce and Covenantal Love," this volume.

7. Furey, "Familiar Commerce."

8. Furey, "Familiar Commerce."

9. Here I am thinking with Denise da Silva in her magisterial text, *Toward a Global Idea of Race* (Minneapolis: University of Minnesota Press, 2007).

10. John Winthrop, "A Model of Christian Charity," Winthrop Society, accessed February 6, 2018, https://www.winthropsociety.com/doc_charity.php.

11. Winthrop, "A Model of Christian Charity."

12. Hortense Spillers, "Mama's Baby, Papa's Maybe: An American Grammar Book," chap. 8 in *Black, White, and in Color: Essays on American Literature and Culture* (Chicago: University of Chicago Press, 2003), 206.

13. Matthew Scherer, "A Yet Unapproachable America," this volume.

14. Scherer, "A Yet Unapproachable America."

15. Scherer.

16. Scherer.

17. Scherer.

18. For an account of abjection, see Julia Kristeva, *Powers of Horror: An Essay on Abjection*, trans. Leon Roudiez (New York: Columbia University Press, 1982), 1–31.

19. Scherer, "A Yet Unapproachable America."

20. See Lisa Lowe, *The Intimacies of Four Continents* (Durham, NC: Duke University Press, 2015).

21. See Spillers, "Mama's Baby."

II. Fiction

4

"A History of America"

Comments on *Johnson v M'Intosh*

Winnifred Fallers Sullivan

OF THE SUITE OF EARLY JUDICIAL OPINIONS WHICH PRETEND TO establish the reach of US law, there is perhaps no case more consequential than the 1823 Supreme Court decision in *Johnson and Graham's Lessee v M'Intosh*.[1] This decision originated in a plea in ejectment to quiet title to 43,000 square miles of land in Illinois and Indiana, a form of local action that was normally cognizable only by state courts but which, in this case, by virtue of clever lawyering, had been turned into a federal diversity action, and then moved in a matter of months to the Supreme Court from the brand new federal district court in the then brand new state of Illinois.[2] The opinion by Chief Justice John Marshall finding for the defendant concluded not just a by then decades old dispute over ownership to a tract of land; it implicated all subsequent land claims in North America—and well beyond. Virtually every sentence forges a link in the chain that binds the reader to Marshall's complex and brilliant rhetorical violence.

As presented to the Court, *Johnson v M'Intosh* was ostensibly a suit between the successors to Thomas Johnson, one of a group of investors who had purchased land from the Illinois and Piankeshaw Indians fifty years earlier, and William M'Intosh, who claimed to have been granted part of the same land in 1818 as bounty provided to Virginia soldiers who had fought in the Revolutionary War. The narrow presenting question for the district court was whether the first sale was valid—or, in other words, as Marshall put it, whether the Piankeshaw and Illinois had the legal capacity to sell the land. However, also before the Court was the validity of the grants to war veterans, a promise dear to Marshall's heart.[3]

While Marshall could have decided the case by declaring the sales invalid under the Royal Proclamation of 1763, George III's declaration that prohibited settlement of Indian lands west of the Appalachians, he chose rather to use the case to affirm federal supremacy over the states and to comprehensively define the relationship of the US to the Indian nations.

The collapsing of time and space was essential to the success of Marshall's gamble. All of the inhabitants and all of the territory and all of the centuries needed to be brought together into one legal principle that could bridge multiple claimants over multiple centuries across a variegated legal landscape. He needed to say that

> the United States, then, have unequivocally acceded to that great and broad rule by which its civilized inhabitants now hold this country. They hold, and assert in themselves, the title by which it was acquired. They maintain, as all others have maintained, that discovery gave an exclusive right to extinguish the Indian title of occupancy, either by purchase or by conquest; and gave also a right to such a degree of sovereignty as the circumstances of the people would allow them to exercise.[4]

He needed to say that the federal government now had legal title to the entire continental United States.

This was not an easy task, as Sarah Cleveland explains:

> [T]he case presented a difficult conceptual problem for the Court. If the Indians were found to hold legal title to their lands, as full foreign sovereigns, the ruling would invalidate large grants of Indian-held lands made to settlers by the British Crown without tribal consent. It would also eliminate the U.S. government's power to control the disposition of Indian lands, thus exposing Indian holdings to unscrupulous land speculators. On the other hand, a ruling that the tribe did not hold title to the lands would contradict existing treaty provisions that vowed to respect Indian property rights and potentially threaten U.S. title to large tracts of land that had been ceded to the United States through Indian treaties.[5]

Marshall solves this problem by telling a story of discovery, a "history of America," as he called it, a several hundred-year history affirming US ownership of the land, an ownership ultimately grounded in what he calls the principle of the right of discovery. "This principle," he tells us, "was that discovery gave title to the government by whose subjects, or by whose authority, it was made, against all other European governments, which title might be consummated by possession."[6]

In his opinion Marshall recounts in rough outline the history of French, Dutch, English, and Spanish efforts to be the last European nation standing in this contest. All of this history is told by way of background, in the passive voice, to display the extinguishing of Indian title from every inch of land by some European crown acting before there was a United States, the implication being that the US is not really responsible for that extinguishment. The US appears then merely as inheritor of the title acquired through all of this prior fevered discovery. Discovery does not entirely extinguish all of the rights of the inhabitants, Marshall explains with careful humanitarian condescension. The inhabitants, it turns out, still have a right of occupancy. But they have now become, as one historian has quipped, tenants in their own land.[7]

This is outrageous. There are many reasons, however, why understanding this opinion from the heroic age of the Court should not end there. It is much more complicated. And our complicity endures. To collapse the complications into a simple invocation of victor's justice effaces the way in which the interplay of ordinary law, politics, and business played its part—and continues to do so—and the ways in which the very expansiveness of Marshall's opinion carries the seeds of its own subversion, revealing the lumpiness of sovereign territorial pretension described by Lauren Benton and others.[8]

First the complications, and then more about the "history of America." For one thing, the case was cooked up. They should not have been in the Supreme Court. The litigants, all of them on both sides land speculators, had colluded to bring the suit in order to establish title and protect their investments, presenting an agreed upon set of facts to the Illinois court, and thereby successfully evading difficult evidentiary problems caused by the length of time since the purchases. The evidence for the sales was a stipulation which the plaintiffs paid M'Intosh for. It is a sordid tale.

The plaintiffs had also carefully narrowed the legal issues to the one they thought they could win on: the reach of George III's Proclamation of 1763 barring purchases of Indian lands west of the Appalachians. They failed in that effort. They had focused on the past. Marshall was focused on the future. By 1823 it was essential that, as Marshall put it,

> As the right of society, to prescribe those rules by which property may be acquired and preserved is not, and cannot be drawn into question" . . . [and] "the title to lands, especially, is and must be admitted to depend entirely on the law of the nation in which they lie" . . . it will be necessary, in pursuing this inquiry, to examine, not singly those principles of abstract justice, which

the Creator of all things has impressed on the mind of his creature man, and which are admitted to regulate, in a great degree, the rights of civilized nations, whose perfect independence is acknowledged; but those principles also which our own government has adopted in the particular case, and given us as the rule for our decision.[9]

By this sentence, Marshall converted the case from one sounding in either natural law or the law of nations to a question of positive law. "As now reformulated, the question was whether in 1823 Indians could give, and individuals receive, a title that could be so recognized. By means of this second framing, Marshall converted *Johnson* into a case about the validity of post–Revolutionary War Indian land transactions."[10]

The fascinating details of the tangled history of this land claim, the many abortive efforts to petition Congress to affirm its legitimacy, and the story of the collusive nature of the eventual litigation, have been established by a recent book based on newly discovered archives of the United Illinois and Wabash Land Companies.[11] The claimants had been working every legal and political angle in the territory and in Washington for decades. While they made every effort to control the litigation in their favor, scheming to find a sympathetic judge and even hiring famed orator Daniel Webster to argue their case before a Court recently packed with Federalist justices, in the end the case was hijacked by Marshall to his own ends.

The apparently unitary magisterial story Marshall tells about "the history of America," the law of nations, the law of war and necessity, and the doctrine of discovery not only papers over the collusion, it belies and obscures a much more complex patchwork of land arrangements between Indians and various colonial and state governments, as well as with numerous land speculators—a massive greedy effort transversing periods of war and the rise and fall of colonial powers. Marshall was himself a successful land speculator, as many leading Americans were, as well as being involved in a prolonged and nasty political battle with Thomas Jefferson and others of his fellow Virginians, also land speculators. The property theories supporting those arrangements were also more varied, as Marshall himself acknowledges.

Among the larger legal and political issues implicated in this case, as would become clear in the other two of the trio of Indian cases decided by the Court during Marshall's tenure, would become an ongoing struggle between federal and state power. When Marshall later saw how the doctrine of discovery was being used to dispossess the Indians by the states he tried to take it back, insisting that Indians retained a right of self-government.[12]

By then, however, Andrew Jackson was president and he wanted to use the doctrine to underwrite Indian removal.

A further and lingering complication lies in the failure of Marshall's opinion in *Johnson v M'Intosh* to resolve the ambiguity as to what exactly the doctrine of discovery gave to the United States: absolute ownership over Indian lands or merely the right to be first among European nations in dealing with Indian nations. This gap can be seen in retrospect to reflect what would become an ongoing tension about the source of authority for the US to act internationally—whether that power derives from the Constitution or from the "law of nations." In other words, does the federal government have inherent powers in addition to enumerated powers—and what are those powers with respect to foreign policy in particular? This question is first raised in the trio of Marshall Indian cases; again in the late nineteenth-century cases concerning US expansion, including *United States v. Curtiss-Wright Exp. Corp.*, 299 U.S. 304, 318 (1936); and then again in the Guantanamo cases.[13]

*   *   *

Let us return to Marshall's history of America. He begins with discovery, carefully deflecting to the great nations of Europe and the conflict among them the responsibility for the conquest:

> On the discovery of this immense continent, the great nations of Europe were eager to appropriate to themselves so much of it as they could respectively acquire. Its vast extent offered an ample field to the ambition and enterprise of all; and the character and religion of its inhabitants afforded an apology for considering them as a people over whom the superior genius of Europe might claim an ascendency. The potentates of the old world found no difficulty in convincing themselves that they made ample compensation to the inhabitants of the new, by bestowing on them civilization and Christianity, in exchange for unlimited independence.[14]

Masterfully employing the passive voice, Marshall appears to lament but not reject the conquest, seeing it as a deed already done:

> In the establishment of these relations, the rights of the original inhabitants were, in no instance, entirely disregarded; but were necessarily, to a considerable extent, impaired. They were admitted to be the rightful occupants of the soil, with a legal as well as just claim to retain possession of it, and to use it according to their own discretion; but their rights to complete sovereignty, as independent nations, were necessarily diminished, and their power to dispose of the soil at their own will, to whomsoever they pleased, was denied by the original fundamental principle, that discovery gave exclusive title to those who made it.[15]

Marshall then details the New World activities of each European power in turn, beginning with Spain, through to the Louisiana Purchase, returning periodically to remind the reader of the great principle of discovery: "The United States, then, have unequivocally acceded to that great and broad rule by which its civilized inhabitants now hold this country. They hold, and assert in themselves, the title by which it was acquired."[16] But, again the lament, again quickly dispensed with:

> Although we do not mean to engage in the defence of those principles which Europeans have applied to Indian title, they may, we think, find some excuse, if not justification, in the character and habits of the people whose rights have been wrested from them . . . the tribes of Indians inhabiting this country were fierce savages, whose occupation was war, and whose subsistence was drawn chiefly from the forest. To leave them in possession of their country, was to leave the country a wilderness. . . . However extravagant the pretension of converting the discovery of an inhabited country into conquest may appear; if the principle has been asserted in the first instance, and afterwards sustained; if a country has been acquired and held under it; if the property of the great mass of the community originates in it, it becomes the law of the land, and cannot be questioned.[17]

Marshall's effectiveness in transforming the world through legal words is impressive and tragic, as Lindsay Robertson notes.

> Marshall's incorporation of the discovery doctrine into the *Johnson* opinion led to political catastrophe for Native Americans . . . and the United States has inherited a legal regime dependent on their subsequent politically driven resurrection of a wrongly decided, collusive case. Perhaps even more troubling, other former British colonial states have imported the doctrine, establishing it as a baseline for indigenous relations throughout the English-speaking world.[18]

The opinion itself is quite remarkable as a legal text. It is a masterpiece of rhetorical overreach and strategic ambiguity. There are virtually no citations to precedent. Lindsay Robertson says that Marshall wrote it in a week, a week otherwise very busy, cribbing part of it from his *Life of George Washington*. He also quotes Thomas Jefferson on Marshall: "When conversing with Marshall," Jefferson reportedly said, "I never admit anything. So sure as you admit any position to be good, no matter how remote from the conclusion he seeks to establish, you are gone." [19]

There is a sense in which every effort we make to diminish its power only enhances it. One sees in Marshall's opinion the fancy legal footwork at the heart of the American project, one that claims fidelity to the rule of law and to the law of nations while acting as an outlaw, an outlaw whose justification in subjugating savages is in her claim to being Christian and civilized in a new and very special way.

Recognizing the collusive nature of the lawsuit and the dirty hands of the government officials who participated in it draws attention to the jurisdictional flaw at the heart of this case. But it also draws attention to how jurisdiction is effected. *Johnson v M'Intosh* came before the Supreme Court only as the result of a manufactured dispute designed to create diversity jurisdiction in a state which still lacked an independent circuit court of appeals. While there is evidence that Marshall was aware of all of this, he still seized the chance, as he arguably did in other early cases before the Court, to define the Court's power expansively. He does this through jurisdiction, that is by "speaking the law." As Justin Richland explains in his article summarizing law and language scholarship on, and the importance of, jurisdiction, "by attending . . . to jurisdiction, the reader is redirected toward understanding sovereignty as an active undertaking and moreover one that is getting (re)constituted in the unfolding, unstable pragmatics of the present."[20] Importantly, as Richland explains, by attending to language, we are not leaving the realm of the real, we are immersed in it. Changing the history of America is not separate from making the history. Telling a different story would involve rewriting the titles of every piece of real estate in the country. Telling a different story is what Indians all over the country today are engaged in doing.[21]

Cooper Harriss in this collection describes the "Great American Novel" this way:

> The central irony (some may say tragedy) of "America" rests in the notion that its potential ("who we say we are") renders the reality ("who we are") unbearable. Great American novels qualify as "great" because they bring the full brunt of this reality to the fore. As "novels," they offer literary ritualization of McKeon's internal moral state of its people. As "American" they do so through recourse to race, violence, and (re)memory (*Light in August*, *The Sport of Kings*, Toni Morrison's *Beloved* [1987]), the ship of state (*Moby-Dick*, *The Adventures of Huckleberry Finn*), or notable disjunctures between appearances and reality (*Invisible Man*).

Might we see Marshall's opinion as in some sense a great American novel *avant la lettre*? Might we say that there is an earlier moment before the periodizations offered by literary critics (1860s to 1920s) and (1920s to 1960s)—one that reads not the Civil War but the French and Indian War as formative, and the Indian genocide, not slavery, as the original sin? The Supreme Court opinions that conjured the nation, *Marbury v Madison*,

McCulloch v Maryland, and *Johnson v M'Intosh* were in many ways works of fiction. Like the novels Harriss discusses they necessarily fall short, carrying the seeds of their own failure.

Returning to Marshall we see that he legitimates the decision by drawing together in one sentence the "principles of abstract justice which the Creator of all things has impressed on the mind of his creature" and "those principles also which our own government has adopted in the particular case," occluding and effacing the rights and actions of other governments, both European and Indian. He tells a story in which natural right and positive law are (and in some sense must be) coincident with federal ownership.

And yet he also cannot resist adding shadows to the picture. After describing the process by which the European nations fought among themselves to establish who should have the right by way of discovery, with Great Britain being left the victor, and describing the ideal process by which a subject people become assimilated to a conquering culture, Marshall says that "But the tribes of Indians inhabiting this country . . . were as brave and as high spirited as they were fierce, and were ready to repel by arms every attempt on their independence."[22] Marshall grew up on the frontier. He was not a plantation owner like Jefferson. He did not romanticize a rural agrarian democracy. There is almost regret in his assertion of the doctrine; he appears too honest to deny the crime: "However extravagant the pretension of converting the discovery of an inhabited country into conquest may appear; if the principle has been asserted in the first instance, and afterwards sustained; if a country has been acquired and held under it; if the property of the great mass of the community originates in it, it becomes the law of the land, and cannot be questioned."[23]

Harriss concludes: "There are no answers, only horizons. Sounding the distance between internal moral condition and external social order, great American novels provide the unbearable evidence of just what such gods require." We know from the God of earlier periods in American colonial history, discussed in Constance Furey's essay in this volume, just how terrifying that judgment is imagined.

Marshall's trilogy can be seen now to have set the course for an attempt to make Indians permanent, dependent non-citizens, but they also make very large claims about the nature of American sovereignty. It was a bold move, a Schmittian moment of creation, if you like, one of breathtaking originary violence.

Notes

1. *Johnson & Graham's Lessee v. McIntosh*, 21 U.S. 543 (1823), Justia, Supreme Court, https://supreme.justia.com/cases/federal/us/21/543/; 5 L. Ed. 681; 1823 U.S. LEXIS 293; 8 Wheat. 543.

2. One way to make a federal case out of what would otherwise be a matter of state law is to arrange that plaintiff and defendant are citizens of different states. 28 U.S. Code § 1332. For a careful reconstruction of the back story to this case, see Lindsay Robertson, *Conquest by Law: How the Discovery of America Dispossessed Native Peoples of Their Land* (Oxford 2005).

3. Joel Richard Paul, *Without Precedent: Chief Justice John Marshall and his Times* (New York: Riverhead Books 2018), 404.

4. 21 US at 587.

5. Sarah Cleveland, "Powers Inherent in Sovereignty" *Texas Law Review* 81, no. 1 (November 2002): 1–284.

6. 21 US at 573. The principle of discovery was actually hugely controversial in Marshall's time and largely discredited by many European lawyers. See Paul, *Without Precedent*, 403. See also Eric Kades, "History and Interpretation of the Great Case of *Johnson v. M'Intosh*," *Law and History Review* 19, no. 1 (Spring, 2001), 67–116.

7. Robertson, *Conquest by Law*, 4.

8. Lauren Benton, *A Search for Sovereignty: Law and Geography in European Empires, 1400–1900*. (New York: Cambridge University Press, 2010) and Christopher Tomlins and Bruce H. Mann, eds, *The Many Legalities of Early America* (Chapel Hill: University of North Carolina Press, 2001).

9. 21 US at 572.

10. Robertson, *Conquest by Law*, 98. As Robertson explains, "[Marshall] steered the opinion away from the case as pleaded. Then he restated the question: 'The inquiry, therefore, is, in great measure, confined to the power of Indians to give, and of private individuals to receive, a title which can be sustained in the Courts of this country.'" This second formulation of the question pleaded and reiterated the Court's intent to disregard the legal question of whether the purchase was valid when made, and then, by use of the present tense, expanded the relevant (98) time period. As initially stated by the Court, the question was whether the titles conveyed in 1773 and 1775 (the relevant time period) could be recognized by the courts (the legal question) in 1823."

11. Robertson, *Conquest by Law*.

12. *Worcester v. Georgia*, 31 U.S. (6 Pet.) 515, 546 (1832); Paul, *Without Precedent*, 421–23.

13. Cleveland, pp. 248 and 273ff.

14. 21 US at 573.

15. 21 US at 574.

16. 21 US at 586.

17. 21 US at 589–90.

18. Robertson, xii.

19. Robertson, 96, 102.

20. Justin Richland, "Jurisdiction: Grounding Law in Language," *Annual Review of Anthropology* 42 (October 2013): 209–26. Richland is concerned not just to draw attention to the importance of language but to repair the gap between empirical and hermeneutical studies of law.

21. See, e.g., Carole Goldberg, Kevin K. Washburn, and Philip Frickey, *Indian Law Stories* (New York: Foundation Press, 2011).

22. *Johnson* at 590.

23. *Johnson* at 591.

5

The Great American Novel

M. Cooper Harriss

C. E. Morgan's 2012 foreword to William Faulkner's *Light in August* (1932) resurrects a literary category long out of critical currency— the Great American Novel:

> [M]ight there be a category for a text that, while intellectually acute, stylistically idiosyncratic, and emotionally profound like any other great novel, also explores an aspect of American life with such unmistakable brilliance and force that we can barely keep from saying that this—this— is not just a great novel but a Great American Novel?"[1]

Introducing Faulkner in this way, and invoking *Light in August* as exemplary of such a category, we might also understand Morgan to refer to the ambitions surrounding her own work-in-progress at that time, her novel *The Sport of Kings* (2016): a sprawling, flawed, gorgeous, affective novel that proves willfully, cussedly *great*—even if a precise definition of that modifier remains difficult to finger. Like Morgan recognizes in Faulkner's work, *The Sport of Kings* offers a profound examination of big themes (race, inheritance, betrayal, desire) that "signify a reality both universal and distinctly—perhaps incontrovertibly—at the heart of the collective American experience, if such a thing can be said to exist."[2] In the process she saddles the reader with an almost unbearable excess of complicity in no small part because such novels offer, by design, little didactic relief. Concerning *Light in August*, Morgan claims that readers "are never told to change by a severe didacticism. Rather, they are prompted to change by . . . their emotional response."[3] The question of whether sufficient change shall happen, or the degree to which it even proves possible, remains open. The diagnosis requires courageous, creative engagement with a text that fights back, not the passive tears of a sideline observer.

Morgan's foreword proves fascinating because, while it speaks in praise of literary "greatness," through an appeal to an unambiguous expression of American exceptionalism (note that she remains silent on non-US novelistic traditions), this exceptional nature, this "greatness," remains ambivalent. In contrast to an uncritical exceptionalist mode—that notorious greatness to which America should return, "again," for instance—Morgan adopts a critical position. In this way she gestures toward a (Reinhold) Niebuhrian irony, acknowledging national "greatness" to derive from the necessity to come to terms through literary production with ongoing exceptional violations of such greatness—which in turn reify that greatness. "Even the best human actions involve some guilt," Niebuhr writes, reflecting the same complicity that Morgan foists on the reader: "The irony of our situation lies in the fact that we could not be virtuous [as Americans] if we were really as innocent as we pretend to be."[4] Virtue, ironically, requires the viability of sin; otherwise for Niebuhr (and this holds true for Morgan as well), it can bear no moral traction.

Such irony derives as well from Morgan's anachronistic language. Who, in this global and transnational age, even speaks of a "national character" or "collective American experience"?[5] Who—so unabashedly—defends literary canon? Morgan deploys these terms as deliberate, even audacious anachronism. She aims to provoke and, while remaining cognizant of the historical wrongs perpetuated by the terms of such singularity, maintaining the discomfort that uncritical expressions of US exceptionalism generate, I find myself solidly on Morgan's side. How, then, to square this—what I feel, not what I *ought to say*—with better critical judgment?

This essay considers the category of the Great American Novel, and especially Morgan's deployment of it in her foreword to *Light in August* (and elsewhere), as theology of American exceptionalism that, rather than exulting in such chauvinistic excess, tempers it. It does so by representing the profound limits and betrayals of professed "national" ideals in order to explore and determine more ambiguous conceptions of these fraught terms—"great" and "exceptional." Like the Great American Novel itself, such intemperance and excess must be met head-on, engaged in struggle that remains ever in progress in order to prevent their institutionalization as the nightmare political caricatures that they can, if unchallenged in this way, come to represent.

Tracking the Great American Novel

The notion of a—or especially *the*—Great American Novel dates to an 1868 article by John William DeForest ("The Great American Novel") published in *The Nation*. DeForest contemplates "the painting of the American soul within the framework of a novel," a task he reckons possible yet, nevertheless, a fait unaccompli by the likes of James Fenimore Cooper, Nathaniel Hawthorne, and William Gilmore Simms.[6] Harriet Beecher Stowe's *Uncle Tom's Cabin* (1852) comes closest to achieving Great American Novel status in DeForest's estimation because of "a national breadth to the picture, truthful outlining of character, natural speaking, and plenty of strong feeling. Though comeliness of form was lacking, the material of the work was in many respects admirable."[7] Such terms offer a clue to the category as DeForest envisioned it. So do the novels he omits—most notably the perennial favorite for Greatest of the Great American Novels, *Moby-Dick* (1851).[8]

Lawrence Buell, in *The Dream of the Great American Novel* (2014), charts two primary periods of historical viability for the notion of a (or the) Great American Novel. The first, ranging from the 1860s (with DeForest) through roughly 1920, surveys an age of anxiety surrounding the emergence of an American literary tradition, drawing upon both the unsettled identity of "America" in its early republican days (those very problems that John Marshall's juridical grand narrative of America seeks to address in Winnifred Fallers Sullivan's contribution to this collection) and especially ongoing repercussions of civil war. Buell argues that DeForest concerns himself as much with shoring up ambiguities of "reunion" at the outset of Reconstruction as he does the vagaries of literary tradition. Accordingly, Buell notes that Great American Novels in this first period skew toward literary realism—a decidedly non-Faulknerian narrative mode—and focus on socially representative individuals (DeForest's "character," as cited above) who offer "some consequential reflection on US history and culture and its defining characteristics."[9] In this way we may conceive of the Great American Novel as an aspirational project, seeking singularity of purpose in the midst of ongoing trial and error. This is not the Great American Novel to which Morgan appeals.

Buell's second period, ranging from the 1920s to the 1960s, reflects more security in the establishment and quality of American letters, even as it diagnoses the messy state of this union. It was during this timeframe that seven American writers (five of them novelists) would win a Nobel Prize for literature.[10] A stronger sense of literary inheritance also became codified through critical studies such as F. O. Mathiessen's *The American Renaissance* (1941) and R .W. B. Lewis's *The American Adam* (1955), and novelistic technique shifted away from realism and toward "romance," the highly symbolic form favored by the likes of Melville and especially Hawthorne and one more rife for irony. "Americanness" and the novels that negotiated its fraught terms did so through a quality that Leslie Fiedler, writing in *An End to Innocence: Essays on Culture and Politic* (1955), calls "depth and resonance."[11] In this way a canon of Great American Novels both clarified and limited potential contenders to "select masterworks by a few practitioners." Buell lists Hawthorne, Melville, Mark Twain, Henry James, Ernest Hemingway, F. Scott Fitzgerald, and Faulkner.[12] Additional candidates qualify, yet they also owe evident debts to this battery of exemplars.

By the 1960s, of course, the feasibility of the Great American Novel was in decline. Shifts in literary criticism toward critical theory and deconstruction, recognition of authorship beyond work produced by white men and select women, fragmentations of the presumed American "consensus" (Morgan's "national character") that such recognition disrupted, and even changes in reading habits effectively transformed the category, whatever its durability in popular conceptions of literary life and labor, into a punch line.[13] It is into this compromised set of cultural assumptions that Morgan fires her foreword to *Light in August* and follows with *The Sport of Kings*, marking it, among other things, as an anachronistic move, invoking an unfashionable category deliberately to jar readers toward a more subtle and urgent point about the risks of abandoning exceptionalism to the exceptionalists.[14]

Exceptional Exceptionalists

The preparation of this essay and the argument I wish to advance about Morgan and the Great American Novel as theology of American exceptionalism cannot be separated from my own intellectual situation, having recently finished one project on the novelist Ralph Ellison and being well immersed in another concerning the boxer Muhammad Ali. Ellison and Ali both share Morgan's ambivalence toward exceptionalism even as they deploy it definitively in their work and public personae. Ellison, whose *Invisible Man* (1952) ranks high among every shortlist of candidates for *the* Great American Novel, intimately knew the outrageous violence inherent to "America."[15] He witnessed first-hand the aftermath of the 1921 Tulsa massacre as a child and later found himself caught in-between more strident racial factions in America—never more than black in the eyes of white supremacy, yet an Uncle Tom to certain black activists disenchanted by El-lison's level and tenor of engagement with racial politics. At the same time, Ellison also recognized possibility in the promise of the founding docu-ments, which became scriptural in his estimation. The US Constitution—which literally enslaved his grandparents—also established conditions for democracy and thus for Ellison bestowed unique freedom, a virtue without which the violence and exclusion he endured would cease to be outrageous, settling instead into unexceptional banality. America's promise in Ellison's work derives from the "more perfect" prospect of knowing better. He insists upon the foolish hope that knowing better leads to doing better, to living up to standards of liberty central to these founding documents—"sacred docu-ments" as Ellison calls them on more than one occasion. Such ambivalence reflects the irony of a virtue that so deeply depends upon treachery for its own traction.[16]

In a similar vein, Muhammad Ali famously takes exception to Ameri-can exceptionalism in the 1960s, refusing military induction on racial and religious grounds, paying dearly with the prime years of his career and becoming a pariah to many exceptionalists among the American public. At the same time, this very act of exception-taking in the 1960s becomes the ground for his sanctification as an "exceptional" American later in his life and certainly at the time of his death. Having become a champion for religious freedom through the exercise of his sincerely held belief, Ali's be-trayal of supposed US ideals transforms him into an exemplary American, a Great American. He becomes an emissary for the State Department, en-couraging leaders of several African nations to boycott the 1980 Moscow Olympics following the Soviet invasion of Afghanistan, negotiating with Saddam Hussein for the release of hostages in 1990, and representing the US as Olympic torch lighter in the opening ceremony of the 1996 Atlanta games.[17] In this way a figure of dissent against American exceptionalism found himself transformed into its mascot.

The reasons for this metamorphosis remain varied and complicated, but it bears out, in short, the ironic sensibility at the heart of the exception-alist myth for Ali (as for Ellison): that anything "exceptional" in this way must also carry the terms of its own betrayal.[18] Morgan notes tautologi-cally in her foreword that "One reads Huck Finn to understand America, and when one strives to understand America, one reads Huck Finn." One may say something similar about Ali, who became exceptionally American by taking exception to "America." For Morgan, exceptionalism qualifies as both "part of" and "indispensable to" whatever it is we might deem "American experience" or even a "national character" to be. Indeed, she continues—and Ellison and Ali would be quick to concur: this sense of exceptionality, such a myth of greatness, may be all that distinguishes "America" from the "mad constellation of differences unified just barely by a handful of common concerns" that it actually is.[19] In this way Great American Novels become most necessary because they establish both the myth of US exceptionalism and its limits. Thus I want to argue, in the space that remains, that the Great American Novel offers a theology of American exceptionalism precisely because it carries the terms of its own betrayal within whatever redemption it may possibly enact.

Theology as Novelistic Depth and Resonance

Novels—whether Great, American, or neither—bind together Morgan's exceptionally fragile unity-amid-difference described above as a matter of course. In this way it helps that the novel itself—an intrinsically modern genre—bears such close association with American national tradition.[20] One rationale for such uniqueness holds that the genre itself emerges at the same time "America" does. *Don Quixote*, for instance, first appeared in 1605—predating Jamestown by only two years. The novel form flourishes as the early republic comes of age (beginning in the eighteenth century). Herman Melville and Nathaniel Hawthorne's great novels emerge roughly a decade before the Civil War, offering serious rejoinders framed by post-Calvinist anxieties in an age that no longer took original sin seriously—even as debates over slavery, what some call *the* American original sin, augured bloodshed. In the process these novelists become the "true" theologians of their time, surpassing the more sanguine (and "traditionally" theological) ministers Henry Ward Beecher or Charles Grandison Finney who, in losing touch with original sin, focused on the prospect of human improvement.[21]

Buell's post–Civil War periodizations of the Great American Novel as what I call aspiration (1860s to 1920s) and diagnosis (1920s to 1960s) reflect the coterminous development of America and the novel as well, highlighting the epistemological crisis that novels, since their inception, have been understood to address: "how the external social order is related to the internal, moral state of its members," as Michael McKeon puts it.[22] Articulated differently, while we cannot know the relationship between a society and the moral standing of its constituents, novels give us a space to work out what these correspondences might be—versions, to be sure, of Mark Twain's distinction between *who we are* and *who we say we are*—public and private selves, identities at home and abroad contained, and often constrained, by nationalist myths.[23]

I want to emphasize two points here: First, novels qualify as "theological" not because they are god-obsessed (though they certainly may be and frequently are god-obsessed). Rather, their focus on interiority, the way novels foster correspondence between personal and social dimensions narrates subjectivity within objective frames. Riffing on Anselm's well-trod construction (faith seeking understanding), they seek understanding through the provisional stylization of reality, acting generatively, speculatively, and not shying away from matters of ultimacy. Novels therefore concern themselves with the kind of significant specificity that theology offers within the category of religion. At their best, as Morgan claims in the foreword to *Light in August*, novels should not offer didactic positions but, rather, appeal to hard-fought imaginative representations of reality that aspire to and construct broader political comprehensibility.

Toward these ends, it makes sense to return to the phrase "depth and resonance" that Fiedler deploys in *An End to Innocence*. Ellison himself echoes this phrase in a draft for a 1971 letter to his close friend, the theologian and literary critic Nathan A. Scott Jr., writing: "I sense more than I can say, perceive more than I've been able to reduce to form. . . . I read your book and I felt most poignantly the loss of depth and resonance that occurred when a concern with the sacred went underground . . . [in] modern literature. How our efforts to depict the grandeur, [and] moral breath of human assertion are muted."[24] This sense of the "sacred" and its signification of "depth and resonance" bolsters an earlier letter from Ellison to Scott in which the novelist confesses a long-time concern "with the relationship of modern theology to literature."[25] Amid the post-1960s historical pivot away from the Great American Novel, Ellison also detects (much to the detriment of novelistic craft) a tack away from the sacred, away from theological inflections of this exceptionalist mode that remains his métier. Morgan concurs in an interview, reflecting unapologetically upon the surplus that characterizes her taste in literature: "I'm not interested in books that are just clever and well executed; polish doesn't impress me, and I don't care about a merely capable sentence. Life is short; I want a confrontation with high art. I want soul. Great literature rattles the mind and makes the body sing. It's an unmistakable, electric feeling, and too rare. That is what I want." This excess, this resonant depth, is theological.

Second, the "great" iterations of this theological function among so-called American writers appeal to the kind of American exceptionalism reflected by both Ellison and Ali: not uncritical aggrandizement but insisting, rather, that the central irony (some may say tragedy) of "America" rests in the notion that its subjective potential ("who we say we are") renders objective reality ("who we are") unbearable. Great American Novels qualify as "great" because they bring the full brunt of this reality to the fore. As "novels," they offer literary ritualization of McKeon's internal moral state of its people. As "American" they do so through recourse to race, violence, and (re)memory (*Light in August*, *The Sport of Kings*, Toni Morrison's *Beloved* [1987]), the ship of state (*Moby-Dick*, *The Adventures of Huckleberry Finn*), or notable disjunctures between appearances and reality (*Invisible Man*). Certainly, reader, you may supplement this list.

Moreover, Morgan's words prove prescient when American "greatness" filters in the present age through certain noxious tributaries of inscrutable malice—the logical, if carnivalesque, extension of uncritical exceptionalist legacies in the postwar era. To sneer at or abjure American exceptionalism effectively abandons this theology to its fundamentalists. Those who would resist such abandonment, or who even seek to correct the political climate it has wrought, will not find "the answers" in Great American Novels. There are no answers, only horizons. Sounding the distance between internal moral condition and external social order, Great American Novels provide the unbearable evidence of just what such gods require. Indeed, the novels ambiguate and ironize this reality, providing rhetorical and dramatic laboratories for the hard work of resistance—Ali as the fighter who wouldn't fight; Ellison's protagonist rendered invisible by his most visible attribute. Sources such as these bear new urgency for the taking of exception demanded by the exceptional age we now (and always) confront.

Notes

1. C. E. Morgan, foreword to William Faulkner, *Light in August* (New York: Modern Library, 2012), x.

2. Morgan, foreword, x.

3. Morgan, xvii.

4. Reinhold Niebuhr, *The Irony of American History* (New York: Scribner, 1952), 21, 23. Elsewhere Niebuhr cites Tocqueville's recognition of the representative "American" as well as his "troublesome and garrulous patriotism" (28).

5. Morgan, foreword, x.

6. John William DeForest, "The Great American Novel," *The Nation* (9 January, 1868): http://utc.iath.virginia.edu/articles/n2ar39at.html

7. DeForest, "The Great American Novel."

8. Herman Melville and *Moby-Dick* in particular, of course, remained obscure until the 1930s— tellingly at a moment of pivot in the periodization of Great American Novels that follows. See William V. Spanos, *The Errant Art of Moby-Dick: The Canon, the Cold War, and the Struggle for American Literary Studies* (Durham, NC: Duke University Press, 1995).

9. Lawrence Buell, *The Dream of the Great American Novel* (Cambridge, MA: Belknap, 2014), 29.

10. Buell, *The Dream*, 46–47. The winners are Sinclair Lewis (1930), Eugene O'Neill (1936), Pearl S. Buck (1938), T.S. Eliot (1948), William Faulkner (1949), Ernest Hemingway (1954), and John Steinbeck (1962).

11. Leslie Fiedler, *An End to Innocence: Essays on Culture and Politics* (Boston: Beacon, 1955), 196, quoted in Buell, *The Dream*, 48.

12. Buell, *The Dream*, 48.

13. Buell traces the terms of the Great American Novel through John Updike and Toni Morrison's work near the turn of the twenty-first century, but also readily recognizes the exhaustion of the category (60–67). For more on shifting reading patterns (and the mid-century trends from which they turned) see Mark Greif, *The Age of the Crisis of Man: Thought and Fiction in America (1933–1973)* (Princeton, NJ: Princeton University Press, 2015)

14. For more on the risks of abandoning exceptionalism to the exceptionalists, see Matthew Scherer's contribution to this volume. Concerning Faulknerian greatness, in a telling twist, *Light in August* was named by Oprah Winfrey as a selection for Oprah's Book Club—surely another category of Great American Novel—in the summer of 2005. Indeed, Winfrey dubbed that season the "Summer of Faulkner," encouraging readers to tackle *As I Lay Dying* and *The Sound and the Fury*, culminating with *Light in August*. Oprah's Book Club would intersect with debates surrounding the Great American Novel at other junctures, perhaps most notably in 2001 when Winfrey selected Jonathan Franzen's *The Corrections* for her Book Club. Franzen, who once appeared on the cover of *Time* magazine emblazoned as "Great American Novelist," dismissed Winfrey's "literary taste—suggesting at one point that appearing on her show was out of keeping with his place in 'the high-art literary tradition' and might turn off some readers." Winfrey disinvited Franzen from appearing on her show, though the two made nice in 2010, when Winfrey profiled Franzen's novel *Freedom* and Franzen finally appeared on *The Oprah Winfrey Show*. David D. Kirkpatrick, "'Oprah' Gaffe by Franzen Draws Ire and Sales," *New York Times*, October 29, 2001, http://www.nytimes.com/2001/10/29/books/oprah-gaffe-by-franzen-draws-ire-and-sales.html.

15. Echoing Winnifred Fallers Sullivan's question about reframing the American original sin, this "breathtaking originary violence" she associates with John Marshall, to Indian genocide in lieu of slavery, Ellison hailed from Oklahoma—the frontier or "territory" as he called it—and understood US racial violence always to carry the specter of the Indian.

16. For more on Ellison's Niebuhrian qualities—including his ironic bent—see chapter 2 of M. Cooper Harriss, *Ralph Ellison's Invisible Theology* (New York: NYU Press, 2017).

17. Jonathan Eig, *Ali: A Life* (New York: Houghton Mifflin, 2017), 476–77; 518; 523–24. The official word on Ali's meeting with Saddam Hussein is that the US government did not sanction the trip, though one never knows what future declassified information may reveal.

18. Sullivan puts it this way regarding Marshall's decision in *Johnson v. M'Intosh*: "the very expansiveness of Marshall's opinion carries the seeds of its own subversion."

19. Morgan, foreword, xviii.

20. To clarify, novels bear generic associations with national traditions across the board (consider the English novel or the Russian novel, for instance, in addition to this essay's meditations of American novels. In this way national novelistic traditions bear and reflect

certain characteristics understood to emerge from national grammars and tropes. For an excellent version of such thought see Ralph Ellison's "The Novel as a Function of American Democracy," in John F. Callahan, ed., *The Collected Essays of Ralph Ellison* (New York: Modern Library, 1995), 759–69.

21. Martin E. Marty, *Righteous Empire: The Protestant Experience in America* (New York: The Dial Press, 1970), 117.

22. Michael McKeon, *The Origins of the English Novel, 1600–1740* (Baltimore, MD: Johns Hopkins University Press, 2002), 20.

23. Ellison cites Twain in "The Novel as a Function of Democracy," *Collected Essays*, 762. Thus, in a manner of speaking, this is Ellison's Twain.

24. Quoted in Harriss, *Ralph Ellison's Invisible Theology*, 97. The draft in question is for a letter to Scott thanking him for dedicating his book *The Wild Prayer of Longing* to Ralph and Fanny Ellison. The draft is held in Ellison's papers at the Library of Congress. I cannot say if a fair draft of the letter was sent or, if sent, if it retained Fiedler's phrase "depth and resonance."

25. Harriss, *Ralph Ellison's Invisible Theology*, 96.

6

Memories of the Future

W. Clark Gilpin

NARRATIVES GENERATE THE MOST EVOCATIVE REPRESENTATIONS of American national identity. *Identifying narratives* employ specific events and particular persons to portray a pivotal moment or decisive action that discloses the distinctive ideals and traits of character around which national identity coheres. The cognitive psychologist Jerome Bruner provided a thought-provoking exploration of this point in an article for the journal *Critical Inquiry* titled "The Narrative Construction of Reality." There, Bruner argued that the rhetorical force of a story lay in "the emblematic nature of its particulars, its relevance to a more inclusive narrative type." Nonetheless, "a narrative cannot be realized save through particular embodiment."[1] And this embodiment frequently includes not only the retelling of the story but also its ritual reenactment. Thus, Francis Scott Key wrote a poem about the British bombing of Baltimore's Fort McHenry, during the War of 1812, which was set to music as "The Star-Spangled Banner" and subsequently declared the national anthem by congressional resolution in 1931. Still later in this poetic narrative's history, professional athletes have made it the object of ironically reverent resistance by kneeling when it is performed at the beginning of a sporting event.

"The Star-Spangled Banner" is, of course, only one identifying narrative among hundreds in which Bruner's "emblematic particulars" tell a story that purports to disclose the distinctive character of the United States. These stories are by no means the same. They accent different features of national history. They stage different casts of characters. And, as with "The Star-Spangled Banner," even what appears to be the same story has been interpreted quite differently over the course of American history. In what follows, I reflect on this multiplicity of identifying narratives in response to the essays by Winnifred Fallers Sullivan and M. Cooper Harriss, who pursue two different avenues for exploring the power of narrative.

Sullivan has analyzed one such narrative from the legal history of the United States. In 1823, the Supreme Court adjudicated a complicated case involving title to some 43,000 square miles of land in Illinois and Indiana. As Sullivan explains, the suit, *Johnson v M'Intosh*, had numerous ramifications, especially concerning the title of Native Americans to land they occupied and the validity of earlier treaties with respect to Indian property rights. Chief Justice John Marshall, in writing the court's opinion, employed a classic rhetorical strategy by presenting the case as no more than a culmination, which revealed the essence of the historical process from which it had proceeded.[2] What Marshall termed "a history of America" led with a seeming inexorability to its fulfillment in *Johnson v M'Intosh*.

Cooper Harriss has focused his attention on American novels and the contemporary significance of a nineteenth-century category now seldom employed: the Great American Novel. A novel becomes a candidate for this category when its characters and the relationships among them point beyond the covers of the book to some quintessential feature of American society, its history, hopes, and travails. Henry James, for example, set up such a possibility by opening his novel *The American* (1877) with the scene of a tall, muscular man, "legs outstretched" and "eyes dazzled" as he sat on a "commodious ottoman" in the Louvre and surveyed both some magnificent paintings and the numerous young women who were assiduously painting reproductions for sale to the public. "And if truth must be told," the narrator remarked, his lounging protagonist "often admired the copy much more than the original." The narrator further commented that an observer "with anything of an eye for national types" would quickly have determined that "the gentleman on the divan was a powerful specimen of an American," indeed such an observer might have felt "a certain humorous relish of the almost ideal completeness with which he filled out the national mould."[3] Like the legal case of *Johnson v. M'Intosh*, the crucial factor that sets in motion a narrative of national identity is the representational capacity James attributed to his fictional character.

Rather than pursuing a distinction between the facts of the law and the fiction of the novel, I find my response to the essays by Sullivan and Harriss to be guided by the British historian Timothy Garton Ash, who observes that the "adjacent territories of fact and fiction both belong to literature." In considering the boundary between these territories, Ash reminds his fellow historians that "to create the literature of fact, we have to work like novelists in many ways. We select. We cast light on this subject, shadow on that. We *imagine*." In analyzing any version of what Justice Marshall called "a history of America," I want to foreground Ash's dictum that "imagination is the sun that illuminates both" the literature of fact and the literature of fiction.[4]

A focus on literary imagination enables me to engage three aspects of our thinking—whether as citizens or as scholars—about narratives of national identity and in particular our thinking about "American exceptionalism." First, such narratives establish corporate boundaries, determining not only which groups—their ideas, practices, and complexions—are relegated to the margins but also the criteria by which groups and individuals migrate into the identified group. Second, these identifying narratives create temporal trajectories. They draw on collective memories to build a beginning point in the past and, in light of a perception of contemporary circumstances, imaginatively project a possible future. Third, identifying narratives become more persuasive to the extent that they achieve a dual rhetorical goal. Persuasive narratives capture the reader's attention by pointing out a specific event or pattern of events that the conventional narrative has overlooked or ignored. This explicit identification of a previously marginalized feature of the national narrative directly challenges any interpreter who would seek to retell the conventional narrative without taking into account the story's newly highlighted facet. In our contemporary setting, for instance, individuals and groups are actively composing a variety of narratives that explain and assess public monuments to leaders of the Confederacy, but it would be extraordinarily difficult to write a persuasive narrative of the past century that simply ignored the construction and continuing presence of such monuments.

Narratives and Borders

In *The One and the Many* (1997), Martin Marty engaged in historically informed advocacy for narratives of national life that would advance "America's struggle for the common good." Marty pointed out that American national identity was built on numerous archetypal narratives and that the perennial ethical question of the United States has been the relationships among these diverse narratives and among the groups that these narratives represent. He summarized two common designs for narrative construction: "totalism" and "tribalism." The former presupposed "the idea that a nation-state can and should be organized around a single and easily definable ideology or creed." This is a controlling narrative. "Set the songs for a country, determine its stories," Marty concluded, "and you will have power." Tribalists, by contrast, resisted the drive toward dominance reflected in a single creedal narrative, by exerting the countervailing power of their distinctive stories and arguing, instead, that "only the peoples and groups to which one naturally belongs, or chooses to belong, or even invents as new constructs, can provide coherence." The central concern of Marty's book was to understand how pivotal stories drawn from national life were "viewed on the one hand by those who seek a single American plot and on the other hand by those who stress subplots of the contending groups."[5]

Marty's effort to understand the viewpoints of both those who "seek a single American plot" and those who "stress subplots" leads to a third point of view that diverges from both of these perspectives. Speaking as a scholar, he finds more possibilities for advancing the national "struggle for the common good" through receptivity to the plurality of subplots: "if a goal of the humanities is to help the participant imagine what it is to be someone else, somewhere else, then the particularizing and idiographic approaches serve more honestly and are more helpful than those that homogenize." Later in the book, speaking primarily as a citizen, Marty advises that if groups "tell their story and accent what gave integrity to their group life in the first place, they will not so readily conform" to stereotypes imposed on them and perhaps thereby contribute to "some chance that hearing and understanding can begin to occur" within a diverse republic.[6] Marty's stress on the listener's empathic curiosity about other people's stories calls attention to a crucial issue in the assessment of identifying narratives. Beyond the content of the narrative, how does the way the story is told invite the hearer to cross boundaries, in order to engage, challenge, supplement, and transform the telling of the story in its conventional form? In short, Marty critiques the boundaries set by identifying narratives in both their "totalist" and "tribalist" forms. As an alternative, he views the active interplay of multiple narratives, the continuous imaginative reconstructing of mythic stories, as the civic responsibility of all who would make a contribution to the nation's never-to-be-finished identity.

Memories of the Future

Through identifying narratives individuals and communities seek to discern retrospectively the course of events that have brought them to the decisions they face in the present moment. From that retrospective interpretation, they coalesce the purposes, ideals, and values that direct them into the future. The moment of decision thus extends temporally; it occupies time. This extended present of decision-making shows itself in everyday language, when we speak of a judge "rendering a decision" based on the assessment of past occurrences or a person "making a decision" while taking into account its prospective consequences.

Both Sullivan and Harriss invoke two classic literary genres—tragedy and irony—in order to emphasize the power that retrospectively constructed identity exerts in shaping decisions in the present. In the case of Chief Justice Marshall, Sullivan notes the passive voice that Marshall adopted in his description of the steps by which the European "discovery" of America established title to the land. Marshall seems to have lamented the long, tragic sequence of events that set the early nineteenth-century American context, but these particular events now constrained his legal deliberations. Sullivan quotes Marshall's summation:

> However extravagant the pretension of converting the discovery of an inhabited country into conquest may appear; if the principle has been asserted in the first instance, and afterwards sustained; if a country has been acquired and held under it; if the property of the great mass of the community originates in it, it becomes the law of the land, and cannot be questioned.[7]

Caught within a present shaped by pretentious claims and their tragic consequences, Marshall accepted a way forward fraught with moral ambiguity. In an epoch of westward exploration and utopian experiment, his legal opinion expressed a narrative of national identity that presupposed an underlying pattern of historical inevitability.

Harriss turns to the twentieth-century theologian Reinhold Niebuhr to lift up the ironic recognition of moral ambiguity that is tacit in Marshall's text. Niebuhr was part of a generation of academics (representing literary studies, political science, and social history as well as theology) that named American exceptionalism as a category of interpretation and subjected it to scholarly critique. His book *The Structure of Nations and Empires* (1959) analyzes "perennial patterns, recurring problems and varied, but similar structures of the political order," because he had become convinced that "our generation" was tempted to stress the "novel perplexities" of the modern era, especially "the nuclear stalemate" of the Cold War. In so doing, his generation failed in the retrospective task and thus overlooked "similarities under the differences between ancient and modern societies."[8]

Considering the long sweep of history, Niebuhr proposed that a government's power or authority to gain compliance, induce obedience, and maintain order depended not simply on coercive force but also on *prestige*.

Under this term, Niebuhr collected the various factors of tradition, custom, and history that encouraged uncoerced consent on the part of the governed. In the nationalistic empires of the sixteenth through nineteenth centuries, prestige included some universal value ostensibly transmitted through the history of the national culture but which, in Niebuhr's view, "lost some of its moral prestige by that transmittal." A nation's assertion that it represented a universal value—whether presented in religious or secular terms—was, Niebuhr argued, always morally dubious because neither the value nor the community was as universal as the nation claimed. "We are not a sanctified nation," Niebuhr concluded with respect to the United States, "and we must not assume that all our actions are dictated by considerations of disinterested justice. If we fall into this error the natural resentments against our power on the part of the weaker nations will be compounded with resentments against our pretensions of a superior virtue."[9] For this reason, Niebuhr concluded, "our age is involved in irony because so many dreams of our nation have been so cruelly refuted by history." Marshall and Niebuhr lived in vastly different epochs of American history, but they might well have concurred in Niebuhr's appraisal of the fate of an idealized national identity: "the recalcitrant forces in the historical drama have a power and persistence beyond our reckoning."[10]

Rhetorical Imagination

Narratives of national identity project not simply a creed but a way of life. In a nation composed of many national and ethnic heritages, the relations among those cultural inheritances require, inescapably it would seem, a story that identifies their points of overlap. In the United States, many of the most rhetorically powerful narratives have confronted their cultural moment with a challenge that arises out of the generally acknowledged national history. In the twentieth century, Martin Luther King Jr. was a consummate master of this art of imaginative retelling. In his "Letter from a Birmingham Jail," King responded to southern ministers who criticized his "nonviolent efforts as those of an extremist." Pondering the matter in his jail cell, however, King "gradually gained a bit of satisfaction from being considered an extremist." He catalogued a list of "extremists" that began with Jesus, the prophet Amos, and Paul. "Was not Abraham Lincoln an extremist—'This nation cannot survive half slave and half free.' Was not Thomas Jefferson an extremist—'We hold these truths to be self-evident that all men are created equal.'" The issue, King concluded, turned on the goal of extreme acts. Would it be love or hate? Would it be the preservation of injustice or advocacy for the cause of justice? "So, after all," King asserted, "maybe the South, the nation and the world are in dire need of creative extremism."[11]

King's famous letter from prison brings me back to Jerome Bruner's analysis of narrative. Cultures, Bruner observed, have prescribed scripts, and "narratives require such scripts as necessary background, but they do not constitute narrativity itself." A tale worth telling will give an account of "how an implicit canonical script has been breached, violated, or deviated from" in ways that resist and revise the conventional story. In this sense, the most consequential narratives of American identity—whether formulated in the courtroom or on the pages of a novel—are inherently disruptive and derive their influence from that disruption. As Cooper Harriss proposes, "the central irony (some may say tragedy) of 'America' rests in the notion that its subjective potential ('who we say we are') renders objective reality ('who we are') unbearable."[12] If this is the American circumstance, then multiple narratives continuously disrupt its present forms in a quest for "who we say we are." John Marshall's history of America will continue to be written—if it continues to be written—by those citizens, humble before a "recalcitrant" history, who are yet daring enough to be "extremists" in the telling of disruptive tales.

Notes

1. Jerome Bruner, "The Narrative Construction of Reality," *Critical Inquiry* 18, no. 1 (Autumn 1991), 1–21.

2. Kenneth Burke, *A Rhetoric of Motives* (New York: George Braziller, 1955), 13–15.

3. Henry James, *The Americans*, Riverside Press Edition, ed. Roy Harvey Pearce and Matthew J. Bruccoli (Boston: Houghton Mifflin, 1962), 1–2.

4. Timothy Garton Ash, "On the Frontier," in *Witness Literature: Proceedings of the Nobel Centennial Symposium*, ed. Horace Engdahl (Singapore: World Scientific, 2002), 57–68.

5. Martin E. Marty, *The One and the Many: America's Struggle for the Common Good* (Cambridge: Harvard University Press, 1997), 10–15, 43–44.

6. Marty, *The One and the Many*, 110, 224–25.

7. *Johnson & Graham's Lessee v. McIntosh*, 21 U.S. 543 (1823), Justia, Supreme Court, https://supreme.justia.com/cases/federal/us/21/543/; 5 L. Ed. 681; 1823 U.S. LEXIS 293; 8 Wheat. 543 at 591, quoted in Sullivan, "A History of America," chap. 4 of this volume.

8. Reinhold Niebuhr, *The Structure of Nations and Empires* (New York: Scribner, 1959), ix–5.

9. Niebuhr, *Structure of Nations*, 20–32.

10. Reinhold Niebuhr, *The Irony of American History* (New York: Scribner, 1952), 2–3.

11. Martin Luther King Jr., *I Have a Dream: Writings and Speeches That Changed the World*, ed. James M. Washington (San Francisco: Harper, 1992), 92–94.

12. M. Cooper Harriss, "The Great American Novel," chap. 5, this volume.

III. Revolution

7

Revolution as Revelation

Spencer Dew

THE REPUBLIC OF IRAN HAS ALWAYS OFFERED AMERICANISTS SOME-
thing of a mirror—the sort that simultaneously distorts and magnifies.
Tehran's famous street art provides the most obvious example, its murals
revealing Lady Liberty's face as emaciated, dead-eyed, a tortured, dying
captive of the so-called land of freedom. Similarly, the flag of the USA is
rendered such that the bars of the stars and stripes plot out the trajectories
of bombs falling on unsuspecting cities, a trompe l'oeil that lays bare what
the American state keeps largely out of view. Such art emphasizes the United States as a ravenous economic and military force, ravaging the world, a
hypocritical hegemony couching its predation in platitudes about liberty.
Yet it is in its parallels with the US that Iran reveals much of benefit to
Americanists, as well. Iran, after all, is a constitutional republic, founded
upon the principle of separation of powers, with sovereignty explicitly located in the people—again, in its political and legal framework, Iran offers
a kind of mirror. This is especially the case with the afterlife of the 1979
Iranian Revolution—the resonance and recurrence of revolution, as act and
ideal, in the lives of Iranian citizens.

The centrality of revolution in the case of Iran parallels the centrality of
revolution in America. In both cases, the revolution is not limited to a finite
historical moment (1776 or 1979) but is a recurring trope through which history is understood. Revolution, moreover, becomes a characteristic of consciousness for citizens of the (revolutionary) state. The revolution becomes
an "inheritance," that, as Darren Mulloy puts it, is understood and "often
expressed in strikingly personal terms."[1] One facet of such inheritance,

I argue, is a *revolutionary subjectivity*, a sense of self—as citizen, understood through citation of mythologized national history and ideals associated with the founding—that manifests what Catherine Albanese calls the "mainstream national consciousness lived under the canopy of the myth of Revolution."[2]

Citizens of both Iran and the United States display such a revolutionary subjectivity, with revolution approached as both particular and eternal, a matter of a ragtag band of patriots in a specific period, for instance, but also and more importantly of universal ideals of freedom versus tyranny. Ideology is always prioritized over economics, the intellectual and devotional aspects of revolution placed above other, more practical concerns as history is transformed into myth. Similarly, the citizen, as a specific legal and political status, is less important than the romantic understanding of citizenship as an ongoing engagement in revolution.

Ayatollah Ruhollah Musavi Khomeini's posthumous address to the citizens of the republic he helped found offers a striking case study in the articulation—and creation—of a revolutionary subjectivity.[3] This text offers a useful mirror for Americanists by magnifying some aspects—popular sovereignty, an eschatological understanding of citizenship and the project of the state, revolution itself as an ongoing process requiring citizens' participation and a universal goal for the oppressed around the world—while also grounding such notions in a specific register alien to the American project—not only an explicitly Shia Islamic symbolic vocabulary and sense of sacred history but also a language that foregrounds religion as such. Khomeini eschews the sleight of hand that repackages "good religion" as acceptable within a secular framework and, instead, insists that religion and politics are necessarily one and the same, what he calls "politico-religious."

Indeed, Khomeini identifies such division between religion and politics as key to political oppression and the suppression of true religion. Conceiving of religion and politics as separate is a global problem—one which can lead to "the downfall of the religion"—for which revolution is the necessary solution. Revolution, then, involves recognizing the politico-religious and embracing it under the banner of true religion, Islam. Within Khomeini's larger narrative of history, Islam has become subject to the corruption that previous prophetic messages were subject to in the Qur'an's own historical narrative. The revolution thus replicates the revelation, as the present *jahiliyya* (in which tyrants insist that religion and politics are seen as separate categories) demands a correction, a return to truth. Shia history likewise provides Khomeini with a template for—serves as a prolegomenon to—the current and ongoing revolution. Rites of remembrance and collective mourning are read as acts of condemnation of and protest against tyranny and oppression; "cries of lamentations" become the voice of proto-Revolutionary gatherings and the Infallible Imams who "became martyrs as a result of attempting to eradicate oppressive governments" emerge as proto-Revolutionary leaders.

Islamic eschatology subsumes the eschatology of the revolutionary state, with the actions of individual citizens oriented in relation to—and understood as consequential in relation to—a cosmic drama wherein the state plays a role. Bruce Ackerman argues that "Even though the Ayatollah was an immensely popular figure, he had consistently constitutionalized his charisma into a complex structure firmly grounded in popular sovereignty,"[4] yet here we see how Khomeini frames such sovereignty as part of a cosmic struggle, one wherein transhistorical oppression, rearing its beastly head in each age and era must be countered not only by historical martyrdom but also by cries of protest of the oppressed against criminal leaders throughout history until the end of time. The crimes of the tyrant must not merely be condemned; with sovereignty comes responsibility, and revolutionary citizens are expected to act in the here and now—action that comes at great risk and requires sacrifice. Revolutionary subjectivity hinges upon continual re-creation and re-engagement of the revolutionary dynamic.

Revolutionary citizens continually contribute to the birth of a new order via their own sacrifice, suffering, and pious dedication to ideals. Such giving of self to revolution is a universal option, available to all, as Khomeini makes clear. Popular sovereignty is understood as promising a universal model wherein the oppressed worldwide, the "deprived people of the country," embracing true religion and revolution, can "Rise up and fight for your rights" against the tyrants and their stooges, "take charge of the affairs of your country." Khomeini's message is "recommended to . . . the oppressed peoples of the world regardless of their religion or nationality," though religious affiliation, of course, will become corrected once one embraces revolution. Revolutionary subjectivity is, truly, a politico-religious consciousness in Khomeini's understanding.

And so too in the United States of America.

I am no expert on Iran, no expert on Khomeini, but I find his text profoundly useful for thinking comparatively about American dynamics so often identified as exceptional—and yet which, when seen through the mirror offered here, can be read instead as examples of a broader typology, a subjectivity tailored to but in no way unique to the American context.

The revolutionary subjectivity described by Khomeini is distinctly Iranian, to be sure, but also recognizable as a concept that Khomeini's American nemesis, Ronald Reagan, though his politico-religious language was tuned to another register, engaged in and perpetuated, citing the sacred past and mapping out an eschatological future.

Smaller scale examples make more striking comparisons and illustrate the need to think of revolutionary subjectivity as a comparative phenomenon. The Citizens for Constitutional Freedom, in their 2016 occupation of the Malheur Wildlife Refuge in Oregon, claimed that the conjoined moral and political project of the United States was hanging by a string and that only through return to religion (understood as, in Khomeini's term, "politico-religious," as the stuff not just of Jesus but of the Jesus of the Founders) could the state be saved. Wearing copies of the Constitution in their breast pockets, these self-proclaimed patriots took up arms to enact their revolutionary responsibility, the stitching of sacred history to the present moment made explicit on the cover of those texts, where a portrait of George Washington was featured, offering a quill pen to the viewer, a mirror image of the present, physical pen with which the bearer was to sign a pledge on the back cover, "with the original Signers," declaring themself to be "one of We, the People," a revolutionary citizen, committed to the struggle for liberty that began in 1776 and continues to the present day. Surely members of the Moorish Science Temple of America, parading with their conjoined Moorish and American flags, declaring themselves to be citizens of the USA and explicating that citizenship as participation in an eschatological drama of realigning the values and society of the state with its original, divinely designed ideals are not so different, either. Part of the appeal of revolution and its seductive subjectivity—as surely Khomeini and Reagan, as worldly leaders, both knew well—is how easily it can be overlaid onto different situations, how neatly its framework makes sense of—gives meaning to—the political situations of different communities, speaking to the various deprived people and offering assurance that the tyrants they face will not stand forever. Indeed, they cannot stand, for tyranny, in this mythic dichotomy, is the opposite of religion, the "downfall of the religion," just as revolution is the proper reorientation of religion (understood as *true religion*) as central to and inextricable from politics (understood as *true politics*).

Notes

1. Darren Mulloy, *American Extremism and the Militia Movement*, (New York: Routledge, 2005), 36.

2. Catharine L. Albanese, *Sons of the Fathers: The Civil Religion of the American Revolution* (Philadelphia, PA: Temple University Press, 1976), 224.

3. Ayatollah Ruhollah Musavi Khomeini, *The Last Message* (Tehran: The Institute for Compilation and Publication of Imam Khomeini's Works [International Affairs Department], 2011), http://en.imam-khomeini.ir/en/c5_3154/Book/English/The_Last_Message. Unattributed quotes here refer to this work.

4. Bruce Ackerman, *Revolutionary Constitutions: Charismatic Leadership and the Rule of Law* (Cambridge, MA: Belknap Press, 2019), 341.

8

Exceptional Americanism

Noah Salomon

IN HIS *WARNING FROM THE PROPHET IN 1928*, NOBLE DREW ALI, founder of the Moorish Science Temple of America movement, makes an eager plea for inclusion of his community into the constitutional and cultural framework of the American legal order.[1] My colleague Spencer Dew describes this plea as far from a revolutionary reimagining of the status quo, characterizing it instead as a prophetic call for inclusion of his people within the status quo. Drew Ali's recognition that black Americans, present for generations, were and, without his intervention always would be, never fully American (or, as he puts it, only Americans by granted privilege, not by right), while people coming from the most far off and exotic lands had a clear path to full citizenship in the American assimilatory promise, motivated the strategy he advocates in this short essay. Drew Ali calls on his community to define itself on the basis of nationality (as Moors) rather than race (as Negros).[2] Such a strategy not only recognizes the essential and indelible place of race in the American legal experiment (then under the shadow of Jim Crow, now in the documented bias in incarceration rates and police violence against unarmed civilians), over and above any other category of human belonging, but offers a way of unthinking it: to insist that race is a construct and to call on his people to adopt a new identity based on nationality and religion.

The case of Noble Drew Ali impresses on us that, in our discussion of American exceptionalism, we need not only to look at how America frames itself as an exception—this is clear from its stance on everything from its nuclear policy to its attitude toward international law to the intense localism of its media and entertainment consumption—but at how that which is excepted from the American promise pushes back, in often surprising ways. For Drew Ali, this process of embodying what I call "exceptional Americanism"—the exception seeking to enter into that from which it has been excepted—took place through redefining black Americans as a nationality, rather than a race, and thus aspiring to become one among many immigrant groups entering into the melting pot. In doing so, he not only sought to unsettle the place of the exception to American political life, rejecting its racialized premises, but also pushed back against the scientific conclusions of the day by insisting that there is no race but the human race. Uday Mehta has argued that liberalism works through perpetuating a tension between universal promise and a system that delineates exceptions—those people who are not yet ready for the liberal gift. In the American story, slavery and manifest destiny constitute the two founding exceptions to the liberal promise. Though some might read Drew Ali's essay as simply blaming black Americans for the oppression they faced, through, as he puts it, their refusal to state their "free national names,"[3] I want to suggest that his agenda is more radical, attempting, as he does, to redefine the very categories through which his community has been interpolated. It is for this reason that Drew Ali so vociferously rejects the fourteenth and fifteenth amendments to the Constitution, which, though they granted black Americans rights, did so within the framework of race: "the right of citizens of the United States to vote shall not be denied or abridged . . . on account of race, color, or previous condition of servitude." Rejecting the categorization of his people by race allows Drew Ali to define his community on its own terms: less the historical Moors of the Maghreb than a creative synthesis of the multiple components of the African American experience and twentieth-century esotericism, projected onto a new image of nationhood.

Though it is understated in Drew Ali's essay, we cannot forget that the Moorish Science Temple not only espoused a nationality but a religion too ("they are to claim their own free national name and religion"), one that Peter Lamborn Wilson has described as "Americanizing the prophetic spirit . . . with a kind of folk Sufism."[4] Refusing narratives that see Drew Ali's connection to the Islam he claimed as tenuous at best, Wilson speculates on a legible connection to the broader Islamic world from sources as diverse as Moors brought to the Americas by Spain following the conquest of 1492, to the Ismaili-Knights Templar pacts (whose wisdom was passed down by the Masons), to the alleged discipleship of Drew Ali's parents under Muslim reformer Jamal al-Din al-Afghani and esoteric Sufi orders. Followers of

Drew Ali have at times embraced such a Muslim heritage and at other times have rejected it. In any case, like other warnings from prophets, "A Warning from the Prophet in 1928" insists not only on social censure for a failure to reform, but divine sanction as well. That is to say, rejecting one's free national name would not only have political consequences (non-recognition) but eschatological ones ("enormous earthquakes, disease, etc.") as well.

Getting his people "back into the constitutional fold" through prodding them to re-embrace their forgotten identity as Moors and as Muslims seems a striking move in the day and age in which we are reading this piece. That is to say, I could not help thinking of this 1928 example and wondering if, had Drew Ali lived today, he would have emphasized his identity as "Moor." Though technically referring to people of North African descent, the Muslim of orientalist fantasies of the early twentieth century has become the nightmare of the twenty-first. Today's Moors are among those most commonly left out of the "constitutional fold" that Drew Ali sought so enthusiastically to enter, constituted as the objects of persistent surveillance, stopped at borders and checkpoints. Whether indexed in "how they treat their women," in campaigns for anti-sharia legislation, or kept from crossing our borders under the looming threat of terrorism, it is undeniable that the Arab or Muslim in the post 9/11 landscape is exceptionalized, written out of the constitutional order. The "free national name" of yesteryear has lost any potential advantage it once had, as race has come to rear its head at every turn, here in a purported set of pathological tendencies of the Muslim that cannot be unlearned no matter the name of the country now printed on her passport. Take the US rules on visa waiver countries implemented under the Obama administration, which stipulate that those Europeans with "dual nationality" (a term I think intentionally left undefined) with a roster of "coincidentally" Arab and/or Muslim majority countries are no longer granted visa waivers but must go through special security protocols and apply for a visa. Here it is clear that the Muslim and Arab (as races that cannot be unlearned) constitute the ultimate exception to the whole concept of post-Enlightenment citizenship: that nationhood dissolves any previous and irrational ties to race and religion. Here, the Muslim serves as the exception to the rule, never able to become fully and equally European in the minds of US immigration authorities.

Would Drew Ali's strategy be effective today as a means of transcending the predicament of black Americans, in an era of pessimism or even disbelief in the ability of the citizenship to do its magic? Exceptional Americanism is still, however, very much a strategy for people across a whole swath of identities, who seek to justify their exception as part of the rule, to participate in those purportedly inalienable rights the Constitution guarantees that are too often, and for too many, frozen in a state of exception. Drew Ali's stirring jeremiad both offers a genealogy of our present—in showing the frantic scramble to escape the race exception—and poses a contrast to where we are today, when certain nations have been assigned a pathological character, with dire consequences for the coherence of not only America's identity as a land of immigrants, but the entire edifice of citizenship, when Muslim-American is rendered an impossible gulf to bridge.

Notes

1. Noble Drew Ali, *A Warning from the Prophet in 1928* (Chicago: Young Men Moorish National Business League, 1928). Quotes from Ali refer to this source.

2. Moorish Science Temple of America, accessed March 1, 2021, http://msta1913.org /MoorishHistory.html.

3. Moorish Science Temple of America.

4. Peter Lamborn Wilson, *Sacred Drift: Essays on the Margins of Islam* (San Francisco: City Lights, 1993), 50.

9

Unexceptionable Islam

Faisal Devji

INTERESTING ABOUT NOBLE DREW ALI'S VISION OF AFRICANS AS
pioneering arrivals in America is the way in which it shifts the temporal-
ity of migration. For starting with the Mayflower myth, in which religious
dissidents in England become a free nation following their arrival in the
New World, the conversion of one kind of group into another has routinely
been understood in prospective and teleological terms. In the middle of the
nineteenth century, for example, the establishment of Liberia as a country
for emancipated slaves was meant to accomplish the transformation of a
racial into a national group.

By literally grounding them in territory, these former slaves were to be
released from the alienated property that was their own bodies, to constitute a people defined by economic and other interests founded in landed
property. And by the same token their former owners were to be liberated
from their own racial particularity to become universal and apparently unmarked citizens. From the United States in the eighteenth and Liberia in
the nineteenth to Pakistan and Israel in the middle of the twentieth century, this way of converting a marked religious or racial minority into an
unmarked national majority has been defined by a future-oriented tempo-
rality.

Unlike this history of racial and religious unmaking, never of course
an entirely successful one, Noble Drew Ali's vision is retrospective in character. It seeks to redefine the forcible migration of African slaves into a voluntary settlement by reworking the past so as to endow blacks with a freedom not dependent upon their former masters. Drew Ali's "Moors" had to

become pioneers, immigrants, and settlers, just like white Americans. The term *African American*, popularized a few decades ago by Jesse Jackson, serves to accomplish Drew Ali's vision by equating blacks with immigrants in the age of multiculturalism.

Hannah Arendt had described American exceptionalism in precisely these terms, arguing in her book *On Revolution* that the republic was able to institute freedom in a properly political sense because it excluded Indians through genocide and blacks through slavery. This allowed white Americans, at least for the most part, to constitute a free and relatively equal stratum of the population unencumbered by the "social question" raised by the poverty and inequality that plagued Europeans and so doomed the French Revolution to violence, reversal, and failure.

Compelled to address the social question, claimed Arendt, the French Revolution and its many successors throughout the world were unable to lend the political realm any autonomy, thus sacrificing institutionally stable forms of freedom to frequent social upheaval and the possibility of populist and other kinds of tyranny. Superior though it proved to be, then, America's exceptional republicanism, based as it was on slavery and genocide, was unable to serve as a model for other peoples and countries, while nevertheless remaining an ideal founded on crime.

But as the example of Noble Drew Ali illustrates, the American exception continues to provide a model for its victims in a quite novel way. From the Moorish appropriation of freedom as agential choice, to the Nation of Islam's ideology of internal migration in order to create a black Muslim nation within the United States, this New World history of freedom has managed to leave behind the violence and racial exclusion of its predecessor, and in doing so has perhaps lent credence to Arendt's contention of its superiority as a political idea.

If the eighteenth century revolutions in America and France were led or inherited by the bourgeoisie, and the twentieth century ones in Russia and China by the peasantry and proletariat, how might we describe the Iranian Revolution that arguably represents their only world-historical successor? Foreshadowing the end of the Cold War only a decade later, and so the passing into history of the class subjects of its revolutionary predecessors, I want to argue that Iran began a new historical sequence and so constitutes the true exception in revolutionary politics.

Of course the Islamic Revolution made plentiful references to its predecessors, claiming to defend the interests of the poor and oppressed against both feudal and bourgeois forms of tyranny. And yet it firmly subordinated economic factors to the purely intellectual, ideological, or indeed devotional ones represented by religion. And in this sense Iran opened up the revolutionary idea to a strictly philosophical reading of politics, one for which ideas or beliefs were the final determination.

This can be seen in the revolution's curiously centrist class position, which its leaders routinely situated between the US and USSR initially, and after the Cold War, between the United States or Israel and Saudi Arabia (or the great and little Satans as Khomeini would call them). The "moderation" or "middle way" that Iran represented in such dualistic narratives suggests nothing so much as the political and conceptual marginalization of economic factors in its revolution. And in this way Iran might well have escaped the dominance of Arendt's social question to become the American Revolution's true heir.

Yet the language of non-exception hammered out not only by the Islamic Revolution's "middle path" rhetoric, but also by its nonhistorical invocations of the eternal and conjoined character of prior revolutionary struggles the world over, deliberately eschews the theology of American exceptionalism—itself premised, as we have seen, on the disavowal of slavery and genocide. And I want to suggest that this denial of exceptionality indicates something more profound about the nature of sovereignty.

Carl Schmitt had famously defined sovereignty in the modern state as the ability and indeed authority to decide upon the exception, by which he meant the potential and on occasion actual power to suspend the norm or everyday legal order and its various freedoms. The sovereign was exceptional not only in the ability to suspend the norm, but also because the position both inside and outside the law constituted a scission that prevented the juridical closure of any political order, and in this paradoxical way made possible its freedom and protection.

For Schmitt, sovereignty was theological because it was absolute and transcended the very law it authorized. Its peremptory nature, so much like a divine command, suspended the everyday legal order based on human planning, utility, and flourishing like a miracle breaking into quotidian life from the outside. In Iran, however, it is the everyday legal order that possesses divine authority and is absolute, eternal, and independent of any argument from utility. And it is the sovereign exception that interrupts sacred law with its purely human and therefore temporary injunctions based on expediency rather than emergency.

The legal principle allowing for the law's suspension is called *maslahat* or expediency. While it might be linked with another, *zarurat,* or necessity, the principle of expediency is not defined in terms of constitutional crisis and does not therefore possess the inevitability that is a quality of divine law. Instead sovereignty is understood in terms of human choice and so freedom. The emergency measures that manifest sovereign power for Schmitt, in other words, may in Iran be considered not an exception so much as a return to divine law, one accomplished by the abandonment of expediency as a purely human or non-theological form of sovereignty.

This apparently reversed form of the sovereign exception emerges from the critique of its European counterpart among movements as diverse as anarchism, communism and, in Asia and Africa, Gandhian non-violence and Islamism. Related to and referencing each other, these movements outside the West identified sovereignty with Satan (as both Gandhi and Khomeini did) and linked even its liberal forms in Europe and America with colonial expropriation elsewhere, just as Arendt argued that the equality permitting the American Revolution to institute freedom was based upon slavery and genocide.

The problem facing these movements was how to found a polity without sovereignty. Islamists like Pakistan's Mawdudi recognized sovereignty's theological character but argued that for this reason it could only be perverted in human hands. The distance between the absolute power that Bodin or Hobbes gave to the sovereign in theory and its much reduced political reality, claimed Mawdudi, opened up a gap in which such power could never match up to its ideal and so made way for tyranny. By reserving sovereignty to God, it could be renounced and a self-governing society brought into being in its absence.

If for anarchists and Gandhians the renunciation of sovereignty resulted in visions of a stateless society, for communists and Islamists the state was crucial for an initial period, to consolidate their gains under a category like the "dictatorship of the proletariat". Mawdudi thought that the very archaism of the sacred law made it irreducible to the political logic of the modern state, premised as this was upon utility and necessity. Sacred law was additionally in the control of religious authorities based outside this state in society. The law, therefore, represented a social rather than properly political entity, whose task was to limit and roll back the power of the state by denying its sovereignty.

But by refusing to vest sovereignty institutionally, as for instance is the case with the Pakistani constitution, which reserves it for God—not least as a consequence of Mawdudi's efforts—it remains untethered and comes back to haunt a state that has ostensibly abandoned it. In some sense, and whatever their purely instrumental causes, the frequency of military and other coups (such as those exercised by mass mobilizations on religious grounds) in Pakistan signals the illicit return of sovereignty to a state that cannot do without it, but has disabled its constitutional authorities from exercising such power.

As if taking warning from the fate of Pakistan, which was the world's first Islamic republic, its second iteration in Iran did entail the institution of sovereignty. This occurred within a complex constitutional arrangement where the separation of powers meant that the Supreme Leader represented not the state but a society defined by sacred law as a universal and eternal entity transcending the state. Sovereignty, therefore, consisted in the exceptional interpretation and even indefinite (but in theory always temporary) suspension of this law for reasons of human expediency and in the name of the state.

Returning to Arendt's formulation, we can say that the Iranian conception of sovereignty is secular insofar as it is meant to address the "social question" by way of expediency. It therefore leaves the law eternal and untouched as a set of ideas and arguments conceptually detached from the principles of utility, necessity, and human flourishing, all of which it nevertheless incorporated *a priori*. In this sense the sacred law, like the US Constitution, institutes and preserves the freedom and autonomy of the political order.

While Khomeini, like Mawdudi, frequently proclaimed the union of religion and politics, his theory of sovereignty does just the opposite. In his political testament, Khomeini recalls a tradition from the Prophet stating that he left behind two trusts, the Koran and his successors the Imams. Forever linked, these trusts would nevertheless remain separated by tyranny and unbelief until the Day of Judgment. But this separation meant that no theocratic order was possible. And it was this indefinite if temporary deferral that made human freedom and sovereignty possible until the messiah's return.

IV. Commerce

10

The America-Game

Elizabeth Shakman Hurd

> *The concept of religion which has served Christianity well
> cannot remain the stable, much less the privileged, lens
> through which we examine Christianity "itself."*
>
> —Gil Anidjar, "Christianity, Christianities, Christian" (42)

IN *TO SERVE GOD AND WAL-MART: THE MAKING OF CHRISTIAN FREE Enterprise*, labor historian Bethany Moreton describes the rise of the Wal-Mart model of Christian free enterprise. This moral reform project tapped into a deep reservoir of need, hope, faith, trust, and anxiety in the communities in which it flourished. Moreton describes the moral and gender economies in which the Wal-Mart model took root. She discusses Wal-Mart's foray into Latin America in the heady post-Cold War 1990s, emboldened by "a fertile cross-pollination of military, commercial, and evangelical interests in US foreign policy."[1] For many Americans this is a deeply familiar story, so familiar that it can be difficult to step back and see a bigger picture. This chapter considers theologies of American exceptionalism as refracted through Moreton's account of Wal-Mart's Christian free enterprise, Winnifred Sullivan's book *Prison Religion: Faith-Based Reform and the Constitution*, and Lisa Sideris's paired essay in this volume on techno-exceptionalism. I explore how the Janus-faced capacities of Protestant forms to both be and not be "religious," an important feature of American exceptionalism, are expressed in these contexts.

When I first read Moreton, I had recently taught Winnifred Sullivan's *Prison Religion*. The latter reflects on her experience as an expert witness in a legal challenge to an Iowa prison ministry program. In reading these books side by side I was struck by the extent to which Sullivan's argument about the impossibility of US disestablishment in the Iowa prison case illuminates Wal-Mart's capacity to both be and not be "religious," marking the corporation as so quintessentially American. Reading the books together clarified what I now understand as a productive ambiguity surrounding Christianity that threads quietly through Moreton's text but is obscured by her easy invocation of the modifier "Christian" in "Christian free enterprise." It is not only Moreton. An unfounded certainty concerning what is or is not Christian pervades American public discourse. References to Christianity tend to confuse as much as they clarify.

While Sullivan and Moreton offer sophisticated correctives to this tendency, most Americans and America-watchers cling to outdated assumptions about the boundaries between the political, the religious, and the economic. The Janus-faced capacities of Protestant forms to both be and not be religious are easy to miss. This productive ambivalence both affirms and naturalizes what Jothie Rajah describes as "an affective conviction in the United States as transcendent."[2] I am interested in the religious politics of these affective convictions. As Nadia Marzouki writes, "to invoke affective feelings is to propose a ritualist vision of the community, one founded on a mimicry of feelings and ways of life."[3]

* * *

Asked at a prayer breakfast whether Wal-Mart was a Christian company, former Wal-Mart executive Don Soderquist replied, "No, but the basis of our decisions was the values of Scripture."[4] Interestingly, in her ethnographic work, Moreton finds that "for most of its life the company did not lay any claim to a Christian identity." Rather, she explains, "Wal-Mart transformed itself into a national Christian icon from the bottom up," with its corporate identity shaped by employees and consumers. "Far from building on or actively manipulating an unbroken Southern heritage of old-time religion, official Wal-Mart came rather late to appreciate its employees' and customers spiritual priorities."[5] Sam Walton and his wife, Helen, were liberal Presbyterians who supported the local offices of Planned Parenthood in Bentonville, Arkansas—Wal-Mart's headquarters. In 1989, Helen Walton was elected as a trustee of the Presbyterian Church Foundation, where she established the Sam and Helen Walton Awards for church development with a $6 million gift.

Like Don Soderquist, most Americans do not think of Wal-Mart as Christian or even religious but as non-sectarian. Like the United States itself, Wal-Mart rises above the particularity of religion. The effect is both to distinguish and to naturalize Protestant Christianity in a particular way. As noted in the introduction to this volume, Protestant ideas and institutions can choose to appear not as religion but as the natural antinomian evangelical essence of America—having gotten rid of all the "religion" stuff. Soderquist's response aligns with this account. It reflects the possibility of basing one's actions on scriptural values that are American, and potentially universal, without necessarily being religious.

This productive ambiguity sits at the heart of American religious exceptionalism and is not confined to Wal-Mart. It characterizes the Inner-Change Freedom Initiative (IFI), the Iowa prison faith ministry and rehabilitation program at the center of *Prison Religion*. Sullivan attributes IFI's success to Protestantism's capacity to shape-shift and be not a religion, legally, but rather a universal system of values. This capacity to rise above the fray and stake a claim to neutrality and universality allows IFI's theology to migrate, though ambivalently and never completely, from the realm of religion to that of universal values. This fluid aspect of the phenomenology of American exceptionalism enables particular religious and political possibilities. For many Americans, "disestablished religion" is understood as a distinctive new form of religion/politics. It relies on persuasion and a free market in religious ideas rather than on state support and inherited membership. It is inherently free, enjoying a fluid and unmarked status. To acknowledge this capacity of Protestantism to be a religion and also to transcend its particularity and not be a religion is a means of access into the phenomenology of American disestablishment.

Like Soderquist's understanding of Wal-Mart, IFI's proponents understand their program's values to be both scriptural and universal. These include an emphasis on freedom, morality, choice, and service to community, family, and nation. Whether or not these values are understood as religious or as Christian is beside the point—an irritating distraction orchestrated by reactionary secularist opponents of a nonimpositional, nonsectarian, and emancipatory intervention. For proponents, the program's moral and spiritual foundations are the product of free will and the outcome of a free religious and economic marketplace. Inmates make a series of unencumbered individual choices. No one is forced to join. Choices emerge naturally and without coercion when barriers to freedom are lifted, and possibilities for material and moral improvement permitted to flourish uninhibited by heavy-handed government interference and regulation. This is a compelling narrative. It is not unrelated to the politics of religious freedom.

Wal-Mart's free enterprise model and the InnerChange Freedom Initiative also resonate with what Lisa Sideris describes in her companion essay as Americans' techno-scientific optimism in the face of the climate emergency. Sideris uses the term 'techno-exceptionalism' as shorthand for the dominant American response to environmental degradation and limitation. This particular theology of American exceptionalism relies on a suspicion of state interference, faith in private markets and the individual, and an unwavering confidence in the potential for innovation and universalization. Americans' faith in science and technology, Sideris explains, exhibits a religiosity of its own which operates at the expense of the natural world and nonhuman life. The Wal-Mart model, IFI, and techno-exceptionalism all traffic in a capacity to transcend both politics and religion. They present themselves as the definition of freedom and the essence of America. Sideris mentions Stewart Brand's famous statement: "We are as gods and we have to get good at it."

It is tempting to dismiss all of this as naïve, misguided, or simply jingoistic, but it would be a mistake. The Wal-Mart model, IFI prison ministry, and techno-exceptionalist responses to environmental threats—like the idea of America itself—are not and in some sense can never be (only) a religion. Each embodies a collective, affective aspiration that is accessible and desirable for all, whether one identifies as Christian or unbeliever, as American or not-yet American, as domestic or not yet domesticated. For Moreton's interlocutors, the globalization of the free enterprise model is, like IFI, "as self-evident as gravity."[6] For prison ministry advocates, any exclusivity attributed to IFI is not inherent to the program but is something others bring to it.[7] Sympathizers dismiss accusations of exclusivity as defeatist readings of their efforts, not unlike skeptics who cast doubt on eco-modernist optimism. IFI, Wal-Mart, and techno-exceptionalism, are not, or are not only, Christian (read: exclusive or sectarian) enterprises. They are suspended in a state of productive ambivalence. They evoke and they efface. They are all the more powerful for it.

* * *

US foreign relations also appear in a new light when refracted through the capacity of Protestant forms to be and not be "religious."[8] In the American imperial project, Protestant ideas and institutions appear both as a religion that may be freely chosen, and also as an implicit standard, set of civilized values, and the horizon against which other practices are classified as "religious," "superstitious," and/or "political," to be regulated and, at times, criminalized.[9] Protestantism is often not understood as a religion but rather as the implicit normative backdrop against which others were deemed to be modern or unmodern. Since its founding, the United States has sought to convert others to American ways of being human, understood both in religious and nonreligious terms. The US government has sought to transform societies in the Philippines and Haiti in the early twentieth century; Japan, Germany, and Iran in the mid-twentieth century; Iraq and Afghanistan in the early twenty-first; and Myanmar, Venezuela and Iran today. Moreton describes the post–Cold War 1990s when markets and missions thrived in a renewed field of possibility with the United States at the helm. Today, aid agencies, nongovernmental organizations, and foreign investors refer to "the Myanmar account" as a "frontier market" and "hot spot."[10]

The American occupation of Haiti (1915–1934) illustrates these dynamics. As historian Kate Ramsey explains, the US authorities there drew a close association between Haitian "sorcery," and popular insurgency. Laws against *les sortilèges* (spells), which were understood to prohibit vodou, were strictly enforced in the name of establishing moral decency and consolidating American control of the island. These objectives were understood to go together. Anti-superstition campaigns against vodou in Haiti targeting materialism and paganism also targeted Catholicism. In Haiti, American attempts to enforce moral decency (and repress vodou, Catholicism, and other dissenting beliefs and practices) were not understood to involve the export or establishment of religion but rather the promotion of universal values, the free market, modern scientism, public health, secular marriage and gender conventions, the rule of law, and religious freedom. This is part of a larger, global story involving the construction of modern ideals of political subjectivity, religion, citizenship, and nation in which hierarchies of race and religion played formative roles. In his work on spiritism in Brazil, for example, Paul Johnson has described the effects of the purification of the mid-seventeenth century category of religion, "a properly civil religion," in dialogue with a "proto-anthropological notion of spirit possession as civil danger."[11]

The Janus-faced religion / not religion binary is also woven into US legal traditions and decisions including the Insular Cases, a series of Supreme Court rulings in 1901 involving the status of the inhabitants of the US territories of the Philippines, Puerto Rico, and Guam, all acquired by the United States in the Spanish-American War. The Court was tasked with deciding whether constitutional rights applied to individuals in these territories. It held that full constitutional protection of rights does *not* automatically extend (*ex proprio vigore*—of its own force) to all territories under US control. These cases helped to formalize a legal gradient of US citizenship,[12] upending the illusion of a clean domestic/foreign distinction, dividing governed populations on civilizational terms, and cementing racial and religious hierarchies mapped onto degrees of Americanness. These gradients and hierarchies retain their social and cultural foothold today in debates over immigration and extremism, police abuse and murder of unarmed African Americans, the ongoing usurpation of Native American land and lifeways, and the dilatory US government response to post-hurricane relief in Puerto Rico.[13]

In *Empire of Religion*, David Chidester wrote that "the enduring opposition between the primitive and the civilized structured the birth of religious studies in America . . . in the US, this division of labor in dealing with internally colonized people was crucial to the birth of an academic field of inquiry that was distinct from but located within the European empire of religion."[14] Haitians under US rule a hundred years ago were not seen as foreigners but as uncivilized and primitive, as quasi-liminal domestic subjects. The same holds for the Japanese and Filipinos under American occupation.[15] Other similarly unstably categorized subjects of US rule—such as Puerto Ricans as formalized in the Insular Cases—were deemed not-quite American, or more famously, "foreign in a domestic sense."[16]

In their co-authored volume *Ekklesia: Three Inquiries in Church and State*, Paul Johnson, Pamela Klassen, and Winnifred Fallers Sullivan introduce the term *churchstateness*. They explain: "'the state' has been often described and theorized, but 'the church' less so, at least beyond ecclesiastical contexts too indebted perhaps to its sense as given. The phenomenon of their often enmeshed and intercalibrated forms—a crossed and intertextual *churchstateness*—requires more detached and empirically grounded description and conceptualization."[17] One might say that US domestic *churchstateness* (our way of doing religion and state things at home) is understood to be free, voluntary, and disestablished, whereas foreign churchstateness often is not. There is freedom at home and establishment abroad. Exporting American churchstateness is understood as non-impositional and benevolent. It would be selfish not to share the good news.

* * *

In his essay "Christianity, Christianities, Christian," Gil Anidjar calls for a shift in attention away from the academic destabilization of religion and toward the site from which the concept of religion was first established and disseminated:

> The limits of "the religious" (to be distinguished from "the ethical" or "the aesthetic") have become more fluid, even porous, most visibly perhaps in relation to 'the political' but beyond it as well. Equally significant, however, is the fact that the very site (in the ethnographic sense of the term) where the concept of religion was established and elaborated, from which it was disseminated, has remained largely and oddly immune to these developments. How to think of such a site? How to call it, even? Is it the Christian West? Judeo-Christian civilization? Is it modern Europe? Be that name what it may, how to understand its referent? If we grant it a measure of integrity (and that is a big if), will it be primarily religious? Will it be political, cultural, geographical, economic, or all of the above?[18]

This requires an interrogation of our understanding of Christianity as (merely) a religion:

> Everything is therefore as if the interrogation of the concept of religion did not unsettle our understanding of Christianity as a religion. A strange essentialism. For what if Christianity were not a religion? Not exclusively so? What if, for two thousand years, it had been more than a religion? Or something else altogether? Christianity only became a religion (in the restricted, modern sense) latterly. Having learned what we could from and about the concept of religion—its novelty, its questionable disappearance, its containment—it may be necessary to reconsider what we mean by Christianity.[19]

Anidjar is right. It is a strange essentialism that allows us to interrogate the concept of religion without also unsettling our understanding of Christianity. To do so is to make visible the shape-shifting capacity of US Protestant Christian ideas and institutions in the sites explored in this chapter and this volume. Using the word religious to refer to Christian forms often serves to mask the protean reach of those forms, reflecting an unwillingness or incapacity to grapple with the demands of the history of "actually existing Christianity" as opposed to what Anidjar calls "Christianity as one religion among others."[20]

Rather than conceive of Christianity as one religion among others, rather than presume that it belongs to the limited realm of the religious (to be distinguished from the aesthetic and the legal, the political and the scientific, say), one might shift perspective and explore the possibility that Christianity, "actually existing Christianity," is a specific series of *agencements*, a multifarious, distributive order (or series thereof) that divides between certain realms (the theological from the political, to invoke again this familiar paradigm), at times creating them out of (almost) nothing, at times unifying those realms and arranging them after a fashion, after a number of fashions.[21]

Wal-Mart's free enterprise model is also a series of agencements that simultaneously divides certain realms (the religious from the commercial or political) and unifies them. The same holds for IFI. "Actually existing Christianity"—the free market of (non)religion and the religion of freedom—enables ecomodernist exceptionalists to become de facto planetary managers, supporting geoengineering rather than reduced emissions and calling for innovations to reduce the symptoms of obesity rather than limiting food intake.

Theologies of American exceptionalism are shot through with an undercurrent of cosmic optimism that can make this difficult to see. As one of Moreton's interlocutors quipped, marking (and making) the difference between "us" and "them," "Guatemalans are so pessimistic, so discouraged. They can't see a Wal-Mart."[22] Denying the prospect of limits, these American theologies—technological, political, spiritual and economic—recoil from multilateral agreements, workers' rights, environmental accords, and international criminal justice. Ceding control to foreign entities compromises the American way of life, impeding what would otherwise unfold naturally as barriers to freedom, prosperity, scientific progress, and the capacity to think new thoughts[23]—all figured as innocent apolitical endeavors—are progressively lifted. This is part of what Sacvan Bercovitch famously described as the "America-game."[24] When it is realized, at last, even discouraged Guatemalans will see a Wal-Mart. Or at least buy a coffee mug.

Notes

1. Bethany Moreton, *To Serve God and Wal-Mart: The Making of Christian Free Enterprise* (Cambridge: Harvard University Press, 2010), 178–792.

2. Jothie Rajah, "Sinister Translations: Law's Authority in a Post-9/11 World," *Indiana Journal of Global Legal Studies* 21, no. 1 (Winter 2014), 137–38. "A paradox marks the narrative of law, nation, and authority in the specific instance of the United States. While . . . law and nation refer to each other and find authority in each other, there is a subversion of secular modernity in one crucial respect: the narrative of law, nation, and authority constructs the United States as itself transcendent" (Rajah, 125).

3. Nadia Marzouki, *Islam: An American Religion* (New York: Columbia University Press, 2017), 26–27.

4. Moreton, *To Serve God and Wal-Mart*, 89.

5. Moreton, 122.

6. Winnifred Fallers Sullivan, *Prison Religion: Faith-Based Reform and the Constitution* (Princeton: Princeton University Press, 2009), 126–27.

7. Sullivan, *Prison Religion*, 155.

8. Distinctions between "domestic" and "foreign" do not map cleanly onto this history. Paul Kramer wants to get rid of these terms, describing them "as actors' categories forged in struggles over space, sovereignty, and boundary-making, the work of cartographers and border guards, the tremendous power of which can only be apprehended if they are discarded as terms of art" ("Empires, Exceptions and Anglo-Saxons: Race and Rule between the British and the United States Empires, 1880–1910," *Journal of American History* 88, no. 4 [2002], 1357). Blurring the domestic-foreign border allows for interesting distinctions to emerge at the edges of categories like "citizen," as when Kramer describes "distinctions among populations that lend shape to its vertical gradations of sovereignty" (1350) or when Michael Graziano, writing on the politics of US racial hierarchies, refers to imaginaries of US citizenship that rely on "a legal gradient rather than a binary of 'citizen' or 'non-citizen.'" Michael Graziano, "Race, the Law, and Religion in America," *Oxford Research Encyclopedia of Religion*, September 26, 2017, https://cpb-us-e1.wpmucdn.com/sites.northwestern.edu/dist/c/1549/files/2017/12/Graziano_RaceLawAmRel-1uypbh.pdf.

9. On the religion-politics-superstition trinary see Jason Ānanda Josephson, *The Invention of Religion in Japan* (Chicago: University of Chicago Press, 2012).

10. See Matthew Kennard and Claire Provost, "How Aid Became a Big Business," *LA Review of Books*, May 8, 2016, https://lareviewofbooks.org/article/aid-became-big-business/.

11. Paul C. Johnson, "An Atlantic Genealogy of 'Spirit Possession,'" *Comparative Studies in Society and History* 53, no. 2 (2011): 393–425; quotes are on page 398. In this article Johnson illuminates the transnational genealogies of the category of spirit possession and its implications for Brazilian "religion," showing how the Penal Code of 1890 came to regulate "spiritism" and "magic" under the heading of public health. "When the 1891 Brazilian Constitution declared the freedom of religion, for example, it was already obvious that the article would not include Afro-Brazilian Candomblé under its protections. The reason it was obvious was that Candomblé and other possession religions had already been subordinated to the Penal Code of 1890, which regulated 'spiritism' and 'magic' in the name of 'public health.' Managing African and other deviant religions after abolition required a re-imagining of the nation, its religious profile, its proxemic rules, and its regulatory style" (413).

12. As Michael Graziano explains, the reimagining of US citizenship as a legal gradient by those who opposed the Fourteenth Amendment meant that the classification "citizen" was applied to African Americans without imbuing them with the same legal or theological protections afforded their white counterparts. In short, "American ideas about race and theology produced a racialized vision of citizenship as a gradient in which some citizens could exercise more religious freedom than others." Graziano, "Race, the Law, and Religion in America," 10.

13. Spencer Dew, "Have It Your Way: Puerto Rico and the Myth of American Freedom," *The Immanent Frame*, November 15, 2017, https://tif.ssrc.org/2017/11/15/have-it-your-way-puerto-rico-and-the-myth-of-american-freedom/.

14. David Chidester, *Empire of Religion: Imperialism and Comparative Religion* (Chicago: University of Chicago Press, 2014), 290.

15. See Jolyon Baraka Thomas, *Faking Liberties: Religious Freedom in American-Occupied Japan* (Chicago: University of Chicago Press, 2019) and Jeffrey Wheatley, "U.S. Colonial Governance of Superstition and Fanaticism in the Philippines," *Method & Theory in the Study of Religion* 30, no. 2 (2018): 1–16.

16. See Christina Duffy Burnett and Burke Marshall, eds., *Foreign in a Domestic Sense: Puerto Rico, American Expansion and the Constitution* (Durham, NC: Duke University Press, 2001) and Bartholomew H. Sparrow, *The Insular Cases and the Emergence of American Empire* (Lawrence: University Press of Kansas, 2006).

17. Paul Johnson, Pamela Klassen, and Winnifred Fallers Sullivan, *Ekklesia: Three Inquiries in Church and State* (Chicago: University of Chicago Press, 2018), 2.

18. Gil Anidjar, "Christianity, Christianities, Christian," *Religious and Political Practice* 1, no. 1 (2015), 40.

19. Anidjar, "Christianity," 41.

20. Gil Anidjar, *Blood: A Critique of Christianity* (New York: Columbia University Press, 2014), 155, 291. Thanks to Winni Sullivan for pointing this out.

21. Anidjar, *Blood*, 42.

22. Moreton, *To Serve God and Wal-Mart*, 246.

23. As Constance Furey explains (chap. 1, this volume): "By spiritualizing newness, as Bercovitch says, Winthrop essentially invited subsequent thinkers like Emerson and Cavell to spiritualize their own novel moves: to depart from the tradition he represented, to replace theology with philosophy, and to associate America then not with a new covenant but *a new way of thinking*" (emphasis added).

24. Sacvan Bercovitch, "The Winthrop Variation: A Model of American Identity," *Proceedings of the British Academy* 97 (1998), 94; Furey, chap. 1, this volume. According to Bercovitch, "the City on a Hill is . . . the first New World ideal to invest the very concept of newness with spiritual meaning grounded in a specific, then-emergent, now-dominant way of life. In that double thrust of Winthrop's image lies the explanation—the how and the why—for its continuing usefulness to the culture. As a rhetorical figure, it derives from two traditions that proved inadequate as the ideological framework for modern nationalisms: kingship and Christianity. Winthrop varied both those traditions to accommodate a modern venture, and *in the course of variation he opened the prospect for something new under the sun, the America-game*" (94, emphasis added).

11

American Techno-optimism

Lisa H. Sideris

Recently I retrieved an old coffee mug from the deep recesses of a kitchen cabinet where it had been hidden by years of accumulated clutter. In faded green letters, the mug's inscription insisted that "Changer c'est possible." The mug is a memento from the three years I spent as a faculty member in the School of Environment at McGill University in Montreal. The message struck me as distinctly un-American, in the best possible way. Un-American in its willingness to concede that things, as they stand, are somehow wrong, and in its prosaic and measured call not for *greatness*, but simply for change. Change is *possible*. It's possible to change.

Belief that the United States occupies a special place on the world stage has driven such notable endeavors as westward expansion, the civil rights movement, and modern space exploration. America's relationship to science and technology, vexing and ambiguous as it is, exists alongside and is inseparable from a stubborn legacy of exceptionalism. Compared to other nations, for example, America is notoriously resistant to the findings of climate science.[1] The United States has the highest CO_2 emissions per capita, yet remains one of the countries least concerned about climate change.[2] At the same time, the majority of Americans continue to trust that hard work, technological innovation, and a few well-timed scientific breakthroughs will secure our bright future.[3]

Exactly what it can mean for one nation—even an allegedly once and future *great* nation—to anticipate its own continuing future brilliance against a backdrop of global environmental collapse is an interesting question. Might there be a connection between American techno-scientific optimism and our notorious lack of concern for the environment? Does persistent belief in and affective attachment to narratives of US ascent somehow hinder the cultivation of environmental values? Does American investment in narratives of exceptionalism make it impossible to halt the destruction of nature?

In *The United States of Excess* (2015), Robert Paarlberg argues that American exceptionalism is synonymous with exceptional excess. Exceptionalism-as-excess sheds light on America's climate policy failures, as well as other ways in which Americans are consistent and egregious outliers—the exception—compared to nations around the world. "Faith" in science and technology, he notes, is integral to America's puzzling lack of urgency on a number of fronts. While skeptical of anthropogenic climate change, Americans are "far more inclined than Europeans to trust that science and technology will provide a response."[4] With Paarlberg's claims regarding excess and exceptionalism in mind, I want to explore the ways in which trust in science and technology exhibits a religiosity of its own that is practiced at the expense of the natural world and nonhuman life. Paradoxically, this form of religion, fueled by belief in endless adaptability, makes genuine change and growth hard to come by.

* * *

My recent work analyzes a cluster of ascendant scientific narratives and their likely negative impact on environmental attitudes and moral sensibilities.[5] Science-inspired myths such as The Universe Story or The Epic of Evolution are popular both within and beyond the academy. These narratives present cosmic unfolding, from the Big Bang to the present, as a modern creation myth for all. The "new story" is frequently touted as universal and empirically true. As such, it purports to inform us of who *we* are, where we are going, and how we should properly orient ourselves to the natural world. And yet, in prizing human intelligence and complex consciousness as virtually inevitable products of telic cosmic processes, these narratives embody naïve faith in progress and may underwrite dangerous forms of human exceptionalism, including American techno-exceptionalism. They may well ratify, in other words, the very attitudes and assumptions, the very narratives of human ascent, that drive environmental destruction and devalue nonhuman life.

In our so-called Anthropocene age in which humans appear to be transforming the planet in unprecedented ways, belief in exceptionalism (of various sorts) and an unshakeable commitment to progress increasingly masquerade as environmentalism. Consider the rise of "ecomodernism," a rebellious species of green ideology that scoffs at ecological or planetary limits and embraces the quintessential fantasy of futurists that technology will allow humans to "decouple" from nature.[6] Ecomodernism is largely an American phenomenon (its chief prognosticators are affiliated with the Breakthrough Institute located in Oakland, California). Emboldened, rather than chastened, by an Anthropocene vision of humans as a geological force that is wholly remaking the planet, ecomodernists believe that all environmental challenges can be met with intensified agriculture and urbanization; nuclear energy; genetically modified food sources; climate engineering, bioengineering, and other amazing technological feats yet to come. Humans are de facto planetary managers. We can look forward to a *great* Anthropocene, a new dream to replace the gloom-and-doom nightmare of moribund environmentalism and its tedious talk of sacrifice, scaling back, and fitting into nature.[7]

Where visions of American exceptionalism once fueled frontier fantasies of discovering and conquering a "wild" and pristine west, ecomodernist exceptionalism embraces the "end of nature" thesis, dismissing previous generations of environmentalists as romantic idealizers of a nonexistent nature. Either way, environmental exceptionalism reveals its bedrock optimism, its abiding ethos of *more* and *better*. New worlds exist yet to be conquered or engineered. More energy to fuel our exploding population will be discovered or created. With perfected knowledge and cutting-edge technology we will engineer our way out of trouble. However novel and daunting our current challenges, the basic storyline—what Timothy Morton variously calls "modernity once more with feeling" or "happy nihilism"—remains the same.[8] It appears we can no longer tell the difference between genuine resourcefulness, on the one hand, and sheer excess on the other. Virtue and vice. The former simply enables more of the latter. In its classic frontier mode and in its post-environmental pursuit of Anthropocene greatness, exceptionalism denies and recoils from the prospect of limits.

Ecomodernist optimism and, to a lesser extent, cosmic narratives of the human ascending to higher consciousness, essentially function as *theodicies*—or *anthropodicies*—in which human direction of the future unfolding of the planet takes the place of God.[9] The goodness that will prevail "lies in the order of things, an order that mobilizes the creativity and resourcefulness of humans."[10] These secular theodicies induce a troubling quietism that embraces the status quo—or worse—and inspires campaigns to facilitate and smooth the way for the future that appears ordained. Hence, for the ecomodernists, climate change presents a challenge, or "trial" to be "met and won with technology," an opportunity to fulfill the promise of progress.[11] This framing of events as somehow a product of inevitable or incontestable forces also enables its *"awed subtext regarding human [and American] specialness to slip in and, all too predictably, carry the day"* (emphasis added).[12] The awed subtext, like the "affective convictions" that Elizabeth Shakman Hurd identifies in her discussion of Wal-Mart in this volume, points to an underlying belief in American (techno-) transcendence.

Hollywood routinely capitalizes on this affective conviction by exalting the workaround: stories of savvy Americans manufacturing the means of their own survival from meager materials at hand are met with awed excitement and rapturous reviews. If the gravely imperiled Apollo 13 astronauts could fix their runaway CO_2 problem with tube socks and duct tape, we have no grounds for despair.[13] Or consider the 2015 hit film, *The Martian*, in which American astronaut Mark Watley, played by Matt Damon, is marooned on Mars with little prospect of survival and few resources. "I'm left with only one option," he casually intones to the camera. "I'm gonna have to science the shit out of this." Damon's signature line is now emblazoned on T-shirts and coffee mugs and shared via hashtags and GIFs (though some engineers felt slighted by the sole emphasis on "science"). Celebrity astrophysicist Neil DeGrasse Tyson was moved to tweet that it was his favorite line in the film.

In its most extreme form, American belief in endless adaptability and resourcefulness promotes abandoning our overheated planet altogether in search of new worlds on which to perpetuate the species. The widely acclaimed film *Interstellar* is a case in point. The film was inspired and co-produced by a Caltech physicist named Kip Thorne who has consulted on other Hollywood films (notably *Contact*) in which interstellar travel takes the form of a spiritual quest.[14] The fantasy of space colonization allows an almost endless deferment of difficult choices here on earth. As George Monbiot astutely observes, "Space colonization is an extreme version of a common belief: that it is easier to adapt to our problems than to solve them."[15] He too notes the political obliviousness or even defeatism that techno-optimism engenders. "Only by understanding this as a religious impulse can we avoid the conclusion that those who gleefully await this future are insane," Monbiot continues. Escape fantasies jettison the "complexities of life on Earth for a starlit wonderland beyond politics." Nowhere is this stealth religion, and its attendant political quietism, so pronounced as in America.

Some forms of techno-exceptionalism stake their claim on the deep evolutionary past rather than (or in addition to) a bright sci-fi future. A case in point is a popular exhibition at the Smithsonian National Museum of Natural History that puts a uniquely American spin on "the" story of human evolution. It tells an uplifting tale of humans' infinite ingenuity and adaptability in the face of environmental challenges. Indeed, charting the salutary influence of radically changing climates on our species's evolutionary ascent appears to be the exhibition's primary agenda. Fluctuations in climate are not just normalized by the Hall of Human Origins: they are revered as a wellspring of human creativity and innovation. Impressive milestones in human evolution, notably tool use and pronounced increases in brain size, are cleverly correlated with periods of climate instability, suggesting in not-so-subtle ways that climate fluctuation has been a boon to our species.[16] The punchline to all of this—and a well-deserved black eye to the Smithsonian—is that the Hall of Human Origins is richly funded by, and named in honor of, climate-denial financier David H. Koch.[17]

Interestingly, the Smithsonian's Human Origins' "Broader Social Impacts Committee" which is charged with public outreach and dialogue, is comprised of American scholars of religion and religionists, some of whom are also intimately involved in promoting the Universe Story.[18] The overtly religious nature of the committee, whose apparent role is to mediate between Koch-compromised Smithsonian scientists and the American public, raises important questions about the kind of religion, or religions, the Smithsonian—or the "Ecomodernist Manifesto," or the Universe Story, or Hollywood—is selling. Religion here is often of the shape-shifting variety described in Hurd's essay. The "productive ambiguity" and ambivalence of such religiosity allows it to work its way into techno-exceptionalist projects, virtually undetected, while also seeming to float above the political fray. We are not supposed to notice that the Smithsonian—whose curator and resident paleoanthropologist just happens to have landed on a theory that climate is a primary driver of human evolution—has made common cause with religionists promoting deep-time narratives of human exceptionalism, and a billionaire fossil fuel tycoon who is bankrolling the whole operation. Having joined forces with the spirit of scientific discovery and innovation, this protean religion effectively naturalizes, depoliticizes, and even universalizes a particular vision of what it means to be human. Visitors to the Hall of Human Origins are treated to a video display of everyday people from around the world and in a variety of languages repeating the passionate refrain: "We are all one species." This spurious "we" covers a multitude of sins.

It might be objected that the Smithsonian's Social Impact Committee clearly announces its (multi-faith) commitment to presenting "contemporary religious responses to evolution." Its form of religiosity is not mutable or covert, one might argue, but utterly upfront and transparent. And yet the existence of this body of religionists, tasked with mediating a "productive" science-religion dialogue between the Smithsonian and the American public, diverts attention away from the religiosity inherent in the Smithsonian exhibition *itself*. The religion of the Smithsonian embodies the spirit of American techno-exceptionalism. It is the religion of Koch Industries: "Challenge is in our DNA."[19] Whose DNA, exactly? Humans'? Americans'? The Koch brothers'?

Whatever else they may be up to, these projects all display an undercurrent of cosmic optimism (or perhaps more accurately, what Terry Eagleton calls "optimalism").[20] Smithsonian curator Rick Potts describes himself as "actually quite optimistic" about the future—or, again, in his deceptively generic phrase, *our* future.[21] Potts cites, as the source of his optimism, our species' amazing abilities to innovate technologically, to be infinitely adaptable, to think new thoughts. "Those traits have never existed in any other organism, including our early ancestors," he adds. "What we see in almost all species over the course of earth's history is that, they're adaptable only to a certain degree." Humans' bragging rights, vis-à-vis other organisms, find support in the exhibition's profound silence—its quiescent anthropodicy—on the subject of how millions of other lifeforms might fare, or have fared in the past, when confronted with wildly fluctuating climates. Should we assume that species that fail to sprout big brains and innovate their way out of climate trouble are simply losers in the evolutionary lottery, fair and square? Endorsement by a multibillionaire libertarian is bound to give rise to such questions. The Hall of Human Origins is evolutionary history as told by the victors: "No pain, no gain."[22]

Yet, despite Americans' putative preference for the difficult and painful path, rarely does our boundless versatility lead us to accept the enormous challenges involved in real change—the challenge of reining ourselves in, of abjuring a quest for limitlessness. Of *resisting* the temptation to science the shit out of everything. Put differently, our "gift" of adaptability is inseparable from American exceptionalism's penchant for *excess*. The truth is, we will do anything to avoid pain. In this respect, cosmic optimism is a form of conservatism—not only political conservatism, though sometimes that as well—because it does not call for change. Optimists are conservatives, as Eagleton notes, "because their faith in a benign future is rooted in their trust in the essential soundness of the present."[23]

Paarlberg argues, for example, that Americans' technological optimism is disproportionately invested in cheap and dangerous techno-fixes of last resort, a "scrambling form of adaptation."[24] In the case of climate change, we prefer (unproven) carbon capture and storage techniques, or geoengineering strategies like solar radiation management, that require no appreciable change in our consumption patterns and aim to protect America and America alone. Rather than reduce our emissions (a.k.a. mitigation), we succumb to the allure of hi-tech adaptation strategies—like geoengineering. Rather than prevent obesity by reducing food intake (mitigation), we seek technologies that treat obesity and its complications (adaptation). "An outlier as an overconsumer"—whether of food or fuel—"the United States is also an outlier as an under-responder."[25]

* * *

American under-response is often understood to be driven by religion, in the traditional and/or institutional sense of the word. Paarlberg points to America's "greater religiosity" compared to other countries, as well as the prevalence of disinformation campaigns financed by the fossil fuel industry, as key factors in climate denial. More powerful than religion, however, is America's trust in "private markets, its faith in innovative new technologies, and its opposition to coercive governmental actions," Paarlberg argues.[26] Yet Paarlberg's implied comparison here—faith in technology *versus* "religious" faith—fails to appreciate the extent to which religion *as* techno-exceptionalism is already acting as a powerful and pervasive force in America.

It is helpful to keep in mind this shape-shifting but potent form of religion when we encounter standard arguments about the relationship between religious belief in America (typically shorthand for conservative or evangelical Christianity) and climate denial, or when appeals are issued for more communication between climate researchers and the religious public. For example, an article in *Issues in Science and Technology*, written by religion scholars, calls on climate scientists and climate engineering researchers to engage in dialogue with religion scholars or religious groups, much as the Smithsonian's Broader Social Impacts Committee mediates between ostensibly secular science and a conflicted religious public.[27] The authors make a compelling argument that climate engineers need to cultivate character traits—virtues like humility and prudence—and they point to religion as a resource for shaping these traits.

Yet the appropriation of mythic and religious language in a techno-scientific milieu is rampant, particularly in high-stakes endeavors like climate engineering, or gene-editing technologies. Hence we find would-be geoengineers, like ecomodernist and lifelong tech visionary Stewart Brand, insisting that "we are as gods and we have to get good at it."[28] My point is that calls for science-religion engagement often fail to take account of these appropriations of religion, and thus fail to recognize the degree to which religion *already* frames these dialogues and shapes the narratives—and the *character*—of researchers. It is not simply a matter of adding religion into a conversation where it is absent.

Recognizing this, scientists and others might learn to draw on religion's resources more responsibly, to reflect more deeply and self-consciously on the marriage that has long existed between religion and technology, particularly in an American context. Greater awareness of the deep entanglement of the sacred and the secular might allow us to embrace religion's potential to chasten rather than simply aggrandize humans and their endeavors, and to claim our status not just as creators but, first and foremost, as *creatures* who exist within a broader spectrum of life. We might learn to make the hardest adjustment of all, namely, to honor and thrive within natural and human limits.

If Paarlberg's analysis of American culture is correct, this will be a hard sell. In America, the thankless job of making the case for limits has traditionally fallen to environmental pioneers like Rachel Carson who reproached the small-minded, power-intoxicated chemical engineer bent on ridding the world of "pest" species at any cost.[29] Carson has a modern counterpart in nature writer and climate activist Bill McKibben who tirelessly promotes an easy-to-remember limit: 350 parts per million, the number that scientists say is the safe upper limit for carbon dioxide in our atmosphere. (The planet is currently hovering around a dangerous 415 ppm.)[30] Throughout his career, McKibben has valiantly advanced this unpopular argument for restraint, notably in his anti-excess manifesto *Enough: Staying Human in an Engineered Age.* But as even he concedes, talk of limits sounds "so negative, so unpleasant." It's like being told to "eat your bran." Who wants that?

> There is something extremely seductive about this notion of going on forever forward, of never saying "Enough." It's dynamic! We'll be smarter, fitter, healthier. We'll press 840 pounds on the leg machine! We'll see in six

dimensions. We'll have eyes all over our heads. We'll have a box that cranks out anything we want. We'll live forever. Pass the ice cream.[31]

The Bill McKibbens among us will always be drowned out by the Stewart Brands urging us to embrace our godlike capacity, our gift for innovation and infinite malleability. Inevitably, "eat your bran" loses out to "pass the ice cream." And anyway, restraint is not the stuff of celebrity tweets or meme generators, or Hollywood blockbusters. It doesn't sell T-shirts and coffee mugs. It doesn't *sell*, period. It may be one way, but it is not the American way.

Notes

1. Cary Funk and Lee Rainie, "Public and Scientists' Views on Science and Society," Pew Research Center, Internet and Technology, January 29, 2015, http://www.pewinternet.org /2015/01/29/public-and-scientists-views-on-science-and-society/.

2. Richard Wike, "What the World Thinks about Climate Change in 7 Charts," Pew Research Center, Fact Tank, April 18, 2016, http://www.pewresearch.org/fact-tank/2016/04/18 /what-the-world-thinks-about-climate-change-in-7-charts/.

3. Aaron Smith, "U.S. Views of Technology and the Future," Pew Research Center, Internet and Technology, April 17, 2014, http://www.pewinternet.org/2014/04/17/us-views-of -technology-and-the-future/.

4. Robert Paarlberg, *The United States of Excess: Gluttony and the Dark Side of American Exceptionalism* (New York: Oxford University Press, 2015), 127.

5. Lisa H. Sideris, *Consecrating Science: Wonder, Knowledge, and the Natural World* (Oakland: University of California Press, 2017).

6. John Asafu-Adjaye et al., "An Ecomodernist Manifesto," Breakthrough Institute, accessed May 6, 2021, www.ecomodernism.org.

7. Michael Shellenberger and Ted Nordhaus, *Break Through: From the Death of Environmentalism to the Politics of Possibility* (New York: Houghton Mifflin, 2007); Asafu-Adjaye et al., "An Ecomodernist Manifesto."

8. Timothy Morton, *Dark Ecology: For a Logic of Future Coexistence* (New York: Columbia University Press, 2016), 52.

9. Clive Hamilton, *Defiant Earth: The Fate of Humans in the Anthropocene* (Cambridge, UK: Polity Press, 2017), 69.

10. Hamilton, *Defiant Earth*, 70.

11. Hamilton, 68.

12. Eileen Crist, "On the Poverty of Our Nomenclature," *Environmental Humanities* 3, no. 1 (May 2013), 132, www.environmentalhumanities.org.

13. Neel V. Patel, "The Greatest Space Hack Ever: How Duct Tape and Tube Socks Saved Three Astronauts," *Popular Science*, October 8, 2014, https://www.popsci.com/article /technology/greatest-space-hack-ever/. The film *Apollo 13* depicts this and many other triumphal scenes of American know-how at work.

14. Director Christopher Nolan inherited the project from Steven Spielberg after he was forced to step down.

15. George Monbiot, "Interstellar: Magnificent Film, Insane Fantasy," *Guardian*, November 11, 2014, https://www.theguardian.com/commentisfree/2014/nov/11/interstellar-insane -fantasy-abandoning-earth-political-defeatism.

16. Lisa H. Sideris, "The Last Biped Standing? Climate Change and Evolutionary Exceptionalism at the Smithsonian Hall of Human Origins," in "Popular Culture, Religion, and the Anthropocene," ed. Lisa H. Sideris and John Whalen-Bridge, special issue, *Journal for the Study of Religion, Nature, and Culture* 13, no. 4 (December 2019): 455–78.

17. Joe Romm, "Smithsonian Stands by Wildly Misleading Climate Change Exhibit Paid for by Kochs," *Climate Progress,* March 23, 2015, https://archive.thinkprogress.org/smithsonian-stands-by-wildly-misleading-climate-change-exhibit-paid-for-by-kochs-bd3105ef354b/.

18. See the "Member and Member Resources" page of the Smithsonian's Human Origins website for more: http://humanorigins.si.edu/about/broader-social-impacts-committee/members-member-resources, accessed May 6, 2021.

19. "Challenge Accepted," *Discovery: The Quarterly Newspaper of Koch Companies,* July 2017, https://news.kochind.com/CMSPages/GetFile.aspx?guid=8781a985-86cb-489c-a7ac-5b4ec39283f1.

20. Optimalists believe we "already enjoy the best of all cosmic arrangements" whereas optimists may see the "shortcomings of the present while looking to a more lustrous future" (Terry Eagleton, *Hope without Optimism* [Charlottesville: University of Virginia Press, 2015], 4).

21. Beth Py-Lieberman, "Q and A: Rick Potts." Smithsonian.com, March 2010, https://www.smithsonianmag.com/arts-culture/q-and-a-rick-potts-6983624/.

22. Christopher Joyce, "Human History Shows a Gift for Adaptability," *National Public Radio,* Environment, July 30, 2007, https://www.npr.org/templates/story/story.php?storyId=12344547 .

23. Eagleton, *Hope Without Optimism,* 4.

24. Paarlberg, *The United States of Excess,* 8.

25. Paarlberg, 20.

26. Paarlberg, 128.

27. Forrest Clingerman, Kevin J. O'Brien, and Thomas P. Ackerman, "Character and Religion in Climate Engineering," *Issues in Science and Technology* 34, no. 1 (Fall 2017), https://issues.org/perspective-character-and-religion-in-climate-engineering/.

28. Stewart Brand, *Whole Earth Discipline: Why Dense Cities, Nuclear Power, Transgenic Crops, Restored Wildlands, and Geoengineering are Necessary* (New York: Viking, 2010), 20.

29. Rachel Carson, *Silent Spring* (Boston: Houghton Mifflin, 1962).

30. For more, see the website 350.org.

31. Bill McKibben, *Enough: Staying Human in an Engineered Age* (New York: Henry Holt and Company, 2003), 211–12.

12

Sovereign Exceptionality

Elisabeth Anker

AMERICAN VISIONS OF POWER SATURATE THE WALMART MODEL OF American religiosity, as Elizabeth Shakman Hurd astutely details it. These visions of religiosity meld free will with a free religious and economic marketplace, so that religiosity comes to entail values of choice, individual liberty, and service, each interpreted as universal values shared by all people. Religiosity in this context, Hurd suggests, is experienced through uncoerced participation in a free marketplace of ideas, consumer goods, and religious practices. This model of the religious practitioner is an "unencumbered individual," freed from government coercions or other external forces in individual choice making, whether that choice is a religious doctrine or a commodity.[1] The religious individual of Christian free enterprise makes self-willed decisions about how to practice religion in the contemporary economy.

Similar visions of power shape the techno-modernist response to environmental threats, as Lisa Sideris richly describes it. In this vision, individuals have the capacity to both destroy the earth as creators of the "Anthropocene," but also to save it through the brilliance of their exceptional technological innovation. Humans determine the fate of nature and can alter it when they choose to do so. They are, as Sideris notes, "de facto planetary managers." Climate change is interpreted as a challenge that can be mastered by inventive minds, a planetary contest in which the most innovative and resourceful Americans will save the human species via technology—a saving that is foreordained. In this vision of the subject, Sideris suggests, "human direction of the future unfolding of the planet takes the place of God."[2]

Both the Protestant individual of free enterprise and the eco-modernist individual of technological progress share a vision of individual agency. They presume a human capacity to control contingency, tame nature, and successfully manipulate the market or climate to transcend the limitations placed on individuals' ability to navigate the world on their own terms. The market and nature are fields where individuals demonstrate their capacity and desire to control their fate. Both types of individuals are shaped by a vision of subjectivity in which people can, if they choose responsibly, disentangle themselves from onerous political and collective burdens, overcome interrelational vulnerability (or in the case of the religious individual, make "service" a way to both practice and delimit relationality), and reject dependence on people, things, and environments they have not chosen. Both individuals, in other words, are shaped by a vision of individual sovereignty. Individual sovereignty proffers that individuals can steer the course of their lives, that their decisions are not dictated by coercive forces external to their will, that they can choose freely, regardless of the content of that choice—be it technological innovations, religious faith, or commodities—and that the act of choosing signals control over the trajectory of one's existence.

This model of individual sovereignty is theological in certain ways. It attributes to individuals traits arguably formerly associated with a monotheistic god: self-determinism, final authority, control over nature, and the ability to shape the trajectory of history. Indeed, it is a presumption of a God-like capacity, as both Sideris and Hurd articulate. This version of individual sovereignty thus might seem to align with Carl Schmitt's famous dictum on sovereign power, in which modern political concepts are actually secularized theological concepts.[3] For Schmitt, sovereign authority in particular shifts throughout the course of modern history from the theological to the political, from God to the king, while keeping the content of final power intact. Yet as Hurd might suggest, in its American formation this version of individual sovereignty moves fluidly between the religious and the secular, and the political and the private. It thus reflects less Schmitt's historical chronology of transferred power than the way that political and religious iterations of sovereignty are intertwined and transformed throughout different historical periods.[4] Individual sovereignty today might seem to display, like the Walmart religious individual, "values that also happen to be American and presumably or potentially universal without necessarily being religious."[5]

This form of individual sovereignty, and its model of universalizable power moving fluidly between the theological and the political but not strictly the purview of either, is a subject position that incorporates both an ontology and a norm. Sovereign individualism is described as a universal ontology for a fundamental capacity of all human subjects. It is, at the same time, also a moral norm that individuals should work toward and strive to live up to. Individuals should do their utmost to fulfill their God-like capacity—a capacity that both is and is not religiously derived. This sense of individual sovereignty as both an ontology and a norm is not new, but part of a longer history. It can be found in early iterations of individual sovereignty, including the works of nineteenth-century philosopher John Stuart Mill, who argued for both. For Mill, individual sovereignty is ontological, as "over himself, over his own body and mind, the individual is sovereign." But he also argued that many cultures of nonwestern peoples do not value individual sovereignty as a norm, so they should be taught, by dictatorial forms if necessary, to do so.[6]

The norm and the ontology of individual sovereignty, as gestured to in Sideris's and Hurd's essays, can be shaped in the United States by a particularly American expectation of sovereignty as a national and an individual entitlement. As a national entitlement, Judith Butler notes, sovereignty is an expectation that the United States has overarching power to determine the course of global politics[7] As an individual entitlement, sovereignty is the expectation both that all individuals are born with the capacity for sovereign willing, and that United States citizens are presumed to have special capabilities for realizing individual sovereignty, in part because of their unique national conditions and values. These conditions include constitutional protections for individual freedom, a frontier ethos of self-sufficiency and fortitude that has outlasted the frontier, and a culture of anti-dependence individualism as a moral and political norm. There is a commonplace belief in the US both that American individuals may be *more* sovereign than others in their success in overcoming determinism, and also that national norms of individualism make their sovereign capacities stronger. It is as if individual sovereignty in the US is exceptional in its expression, as if American citizens are exceptionally sovereign—or at least that they most deserve to be exceptionally sovereign. Americans' sovereign individualism is presumed to be an exemplar to others across the globe. Thus, the American of Christian free enterprise and the American techno-modernist are different examples of exceptional individuals of freedom whose sovereign power reaches its fullest expression in the United States.

This American ideal of individual sovereign exceptionality is some-what different from the (in)famous "sovereign exception"—the power that is sovereign precisely because it decides when it is *exempt* from the law. The emergency powers of the sovereign exception, detailed by Schmitt, of-fer the sovereign the power to both make the law and to grant exceptions to it, in particular to decide when the law can be superseded and the ju-ridical order suspended.[8] It is, as Giorgio Agamben analyzes, the power to "produce a situation when the emergency becomes the rule."[9] Sovereignty, in this definition, is exceptional because it exercises the absolute power to make decisions beyond the law's interdictions. Its power is underived from another source of legitimacy and thus supersedes all other powers, includ-ing juridical power. Yet in the models of American individual sovereignty explored above, exceptionality plays a different role. America's sovereign exceptionality marks American individuals as unique because of an en-hanced capacity to be godlike, to determine their own trajectory, to make uncoerced choices, to succeed in the risky marketplace, to innovate techno-logical solutions to global warming, and to overcome the limits of nature's determinism. This version of sovereignty presumes that Americans have the capability to most fully realize the ontology of sovereign individuality in part because of their deep practice of individualism and in part because they are the most free in their decision-making. Individual sovereignty marks a theological-political-economic American subject who is, simply, exceptional.

This sovereign individuality is a status presumably available to any American (and even any aspiring American) who wishes to enact it, as it is universal in its claims and applicability. It is, as Hurd might note, "in-herently free, enjoying a fluid and unmarked status."[10] It is thus a status, I would suggest, as fluid and unmarked as whiteness in America. Sovereign exceptionality, while claiming national universality, is often a subject posi-tion most available to white people, especially white men. It thus mirrors and recapitulates the model of individual sovereignty throughout the his-tory of western political thought, as Charles Mills, Carole Pateman, and the broad traditions of feminist and black political thought argue, which is typically generated for and by the white men who are presumed most capable of enacting it.[11] The exceptional status of whiteness is clear in Mill's articulations of sovereign individualism, as for him sovereignty is a norm that must be imposed on non-European peoples to bring them into civiliza-tion. In the specifics of American politics, this vision of sovereign individu-ality, while again presumably abstract and universally available (it is, after all, an ontology of the human), is at the same time most readily accessible to the strong man, generally white, who can pull himself up by his own bootstraps, live self-reliantly, remain unbound by others' burdens, master the free market, conquer nature and Silicon Valley, cast off oppressive state power, and innovate a new world. Desires for sovereign individualism are thus particularly strong in the men for whom self-mastery is an individual and national entitlement, and whose vision of god-like control can implicitly expect to dominate over others, especially women and minorities who are traditionally figured more as dependents than as catalysts of power. Indeed, while certainly not the only social arenas organized by these expectations, both evangelical institutions and Silicon Valley companies have some of the highest concentrations of white men in positions of power, and both are saturated with an anti-statist individualism that finds freedom by mastering the free market. The figure of the theological-political white male entrepreneur is the exceptional American individual sovereign.

As prevalent as the trope of sovereign exceptionality is in America, it is currently under great pressure from changes wrought by neoliberalism and globalization, among other factors. As I have argued elsewhere, there are many current threats to American versions of both individual and national sovereignty.[12] These pressures stem from corporate deregulation and transnational finance networks, outsourced jobs and a concurrent shift to a postindustrial economy, dismantled state support for the vulnerable, increased economic inequality and inequitable tax cuts, and the rending of community fabrics and drug epidemics that result from these pressures.[13] Many jobs are insecure in the new flexible "gig" economy across economic classes, and employment retraining through education is expensive and unavailable for most people. [14] Ordinary individuals' ability to shape and participate in politics has diminished across the political spectrum, as access points to political decision-making have narrowed throughout federal units of government.[15]

Yet precisely at the moment when sovereign exceptionality seems imperiled, various subjects, institutions, and norms of American politics and culture are reinvesting in it. There are many attempts to strengthen state sovereignty in the US, including the push for a border wall, the rise of anti-immigration and ethno-nationalist politics, the deregulation of police power, and protectionist trade strategies. There are also attempts to increase exceptional individual sovereignty, which can sometimes work against efforts to strengthen state sovereignty. One effort entails the rise and potency of gun ownership in the US, and the legal capacity to carry a gun in public.

Gun carrying offers individuals a version of personal sovereign power.[16] As political theorists from Thomas Hobbes to Michel Foucault have argued, to have the power to determine who can be killed is to be sovereign over what can be killed and what is allowed to live.[17] Gun use confers a capacity to determine life and death—the power of the sovereign to master fate and control contingency by controlling the fate of others—and thus gun ownership may seem to restore one type of sovereign control. Concealed Carry laws combined with Stand Your Ground laws devolve the power to punish, in certain instances, from the state back to the individual. They boost aspects of individual sovereignty for Americans, especially white men who make up the vast majority of owners and carriers, by seeming to restore a personal capacity for self-determination, final authority, and protection from coercion. This might be one reason why there is a high correlation between gun owners and the subjects of Christian free enterprise.[18] Walmart, for one, sells millions of guns to its customers, and guns are one of the more profitable commodities it sells in its free marketplace. In fact, Walmart is the biggest gun retailer in the world.[19] Walmart doubly bolsters individual sovereignty through its support of both free-market religiosity and gun ownership. The Walmart religious individual and the techno-eco-modernist are thus examples of larger practices across the landscape in the United States whereby many citizens, especially but certainly not limited to white men, aim to rehabilitate individual sovereignty. These efforts counter the felt weakening of individual sovereignty by doubling down on promises of final authority and self-willed control over contingency.

A different effort to rehabilitate the exceptionality of American sovereignty was displayed in the presidency of Donald Trump. Trump's political power lay partly in his promise not only to rehabilitate the exceptional status of American sovereignty—as "Make America Great again" is a national version of sovereign exceptionality—but also in his personal efforts to embody individual sovereignty. Part of Trump's appeal was his self-professed financial self-reliance and independence from wealthy donors, and his general refusal to depend on others, not even for complex political decisions, because it would signal a form of weakness. Trump's performances often entailed domination over others, displaying an exceptionality in which one's uncoerced agency, one's ability to dominate and control fate, entails control over others. Both before and during his presidency, Trump often exempted himself from the law and was seemingly exceptional in his capacity to do so. Sovereign exceptionality, in the figure of Trump, thus led to Schmitt's sovereign exception, as Trump performed sovereignty by refuting governing jurisdictions, rejecting global interdependence, and superseding (or actively flouting) the rule of law. In investing in the sovereign exceptionality of a Trump presidency, supporters may see in Trump a capacity to practice a form of agency they want for themselves. His promise to recapture for Americans the sovereignty he performs was most compelling for those people who have historically invested in sovereign individualism, typically the white men upon whom it has been modeled for centuries. Trump's performances, seen in this light, were thus not sui generis, but merely one heightened iteration of a larger promise across the political spectrum to revivify American individual sovereignty against the interdependencies of globalization.

Sovereign exceptionality entails a promise that both the US and individual Americans can be "godlike" in their capacity to reject determinism, make uncoerced choices, and singlehandedly determine their own historical trajectory. Undergirding each of these promises is a fear of interdependence, a fear that often hinders large-scale efforts to make a more equitable world. This fear entails a belief that reliance on others is always an experience of domination, rather than a source of sustenance and strength. It finds that the only way to be free is to wrest control of one's fate from others, because others only and always aim to dominate the self. Within sovereign exceptionality, collective endeavors and shared projects seem to breed only conformity and passivity, rather than creativity and joint worldmaking. Sovereign exceptionality thus rejects cooperative ventures, multilateral visions, and equal relations of power as conditions of weakness and unfreedom. Yet as global changes toward interdependence continually seem to weaken state and individual sovereignty, US efforts to reinstantiate exceptional sovereignty, both at the level of individual citizens and of the state, may grow even stronger.

Notes

1. Elizabeth Shakman Hurd, "The America-Game," in *Theologies of American Exceptionalism*, ed. Winnifred Fallers Sullivan and Elizabeth Shakman Hurd (Bloomington: Indiana University Press, 2021).

2. Lisa H. Sideris, "American Techno-optimism," in *Theologies of American Exceptionalism*, ed. Winnifred Fallers Sullivan and Elizabeth Shakman Hurd (Bloomington: Indiana University Press, 2021).

3. Carl Schmitt, *Political Theology*, trans. and ed. Charles Schwab (Chicago: University of Chicago Press, 2005).

4. On the transformational practices between religion and secularism see Talal Asad, *Formations of the Secular: Christianity, Islam, Modernity* (Stanford, CA: Stanford University Press, 2003); Matthew Scherer, *Beyond Church and State: Secularism, Democracy, Conversion* (Cambridge, UK: Cambridge University Press, 2013).

5. Asad, *Formations of the Secular*, 196.

6. J. S. Mill, *On Liberty and Other Writings* (Cambridge, UK: Cambridge University Press, 1989), 13. See also Uday Mehta, *Liberalism and Empire: A Study in Nineteenth Century British Liberal Thought* (Chicago: University of Chicago Press, 1999).

7. Judith Butler, *Precarious Life: The Powers of Mourning and Violence* (London: Verso, 2003).

8. Schmitt, *Political Theology*.

9. Giorgio Agamben, *State of Exception*, trans. Kevin Attell (Chicago: University of Chicago Press, 2005), 28.

10. Hurd, "The America-Game."

11. Charles Mills, *The Racial Contract* (Ithaca, NY: Cornell University Press, 1999); Carole Pateman, *The Sexual Contract* (Stanford, CA: Stanford University Press, 1988); Wendy Brown, *States of Injury: Power and Freedom in Late Modernity* (Princeton, NJ: Princeton University Press, 1995).

12. Elisabeth Anker, *Orgies of Feeling: Melodrama and the Politics of Freedom* (Durham: Duke University Press, 2014); Wendy Brown, *Walled States, Waning Sovereignty* (Princeton, NJ: Zone Books, 2012).

13. Thomas Piketty, *Capital in the Twenty-First Century*, trans. Arthur Goldhammer (Cambridge, MA: Harvard University Press, 2013); Zygmunt Bauman, *Liquid Times* (Polity 2007), Matthew Desmond, *Evicted* (Crown, 2016); Butler, *Precarious Life*.

14. Jim Tankersley, "American Dream Collapsing for Young Adults, Study Says" *Washington Post*, December 8, 2016, https://www.washingtonpost.com/news/wonk/wp/2016/12/08 /american-dream-collapsing-for-young-americans-study-says-finding-plunging-odds-that -children-earn-more-than-their-parents; Pew Research Center, "A Divided and Pessimistic Electorate," November 10, 2016, http://www.people-press.org/2016/11/10/a-divided-and -pessimistic-electorate/; Pew Research Center, "How Americans Assess the Job Situation Today and Prospects for the Future," October 6, 2016, http://www.pewsocialtrends.org /2016/10/06/2-how-americans-assess-the-job-situation-today-and-prospects-for-the-future/.

15. Sheldon Wolin, *Democracy Incorporated* (Princeton, NJ: Princeton University Press, 2007); William Connolly, *Capitalism and Christianity, American Style* (Durham, NC: Duke University Press, 2007).

16. Kim Parker, Juliana Menasce Horowitz, Ruth Igielnik, J. Baxter Oliphant, and Anna Brown, "The Demographics of Gun Ownership," in *America's Complex Relationship with Guns*, Pew Research Center, June 22, 2017, http://www.pewsocialtrends.org/2017/06/22/the -demographics-of-gun-ownership/. See also Elisabeth Anker, "Mobile Sovereigns: Agency Panic and the Feeling of Gun Ownership," in *The Lives of Guns*, ed. Justin Oberst and Austin Sarat, (Oxford, UK: Oxford University Press, 2018).

17. Thomas Hobbes, *Leviathan* (London: Penguin Classics, 1982); Michel Foucault, *The History of Sexuality*, vol 1., trans. Robert Hurley (New York: Vintage, 1990).

18. David Yamane "Awash in a Sea of Faith and Firearms: Rediscovering the Connection Between Religion and Gun Ownership in America," *Journal for the Scientific Study of Religion* 55, no. 3 (September 2016).

19. Derek Hawkins, "Walmart Has Wobbled on Gun Sales for Years—But It's Becoming More Restrictive" *Washington Post*, March 1, 2018, https://www.washingtonpost.com/news /morning-mix/wp/2018/03/01/walmart-has-wobbled-on-gun-sales-for-years-but-its -becoming-more-restrictive/.

IV. Chosenness

13

The Judeo-Christian Tradition

Shaul Magid

JEWISH EXCEPTIONALISM IS AN IDEA THAT IS ARGUABLY ROOTED IN Judaism's theology of election, the idea "that God has created a permanent, non-revocable, relationship with the Jews that God has not created with any other nation . . . and this relationship is of supreme value relative to any relationship God has created or will create with any other *specific* nation."[1] The secularization of the theology of election arguably yields an undertheorized notion of Jewish exceptionalism. From a secular perspective, why are the Jews exceptional if God did not choose them? Many answers are offered, from historical ones (Jews are the most persecuted people) to cultural ones (Jews are well-educated) to moral ones (Jews are ethical), all of which are arguably rooted in theological election now transformed.[2]

Jewish notions of secularized exceptionalism in some way share common cause with the idea of America as exceptional, a notion that also has theological roots among radical Protestants who often viewed themselves as a "New Israel" part of the doctrine of Manifest Destiny, a term first coined by John L. O'Sullivan in 1845: "*The right of our manifest destiny to over spread and to possess the whole of the continent which Providence has given us for the development of the great experiment of liberty and federative development of self-government entrusted to us. It is right such as that of the tree to the space of air and the earth suitable for the full expansion of its principle and destiny of growth.*"[3]

The idea that this new land was a gift from God through providence served as an early foundation of the idea of American exceptionalism that is now largely expressed through the realm of a political, or perhaps an imperialist, lens. In one sense, then, exceptionalism of one sort or another may be something America and Jews share, and thus American Jews can find themselves doubly exceptional: members of an exceptional people (the Jews, living in the Diaspora but exceptional nonetheless) living in an exceptional country (America). In Israel Jewish exceptionalism merges the theological with the political more smoothly and thus resembles a Jewish, or Zionist, form of Manifest Destiny which is perhaps more accurately articulated as Manifest Promise or simply divine covenant. In the Diaspora, where exceptionalism is, for the Jews, doubled, an interesting and problematic articulation of what I am suggesting can be found in the ever-popular notion of the Judeo-Christian tradition, an idea that originated in nineteenth-century Germany but was revived, in different circumstances, in early twentieth-century America.[4] The Judeo-Christian tradition is one way the theo-political-territorial notion of American exceptionalism can also include the Jews. Alternatively, it can link the state of Israel to American exceptionalism in ways that we see in certain forms of Christian evangelical Zionism.

Below I examine this Judeo-Christian tradition through an essay written by the Jewish theologian Arthur Cohen in 1969 titled, "The Myth of the Judeo-Christian Tradition,"[5] Cohen was ostensibly writing at a time when "Judeo-Christian" was deployed to express tolerance of the Jew as "other," generously exemplified by the shared hyphen, even as that hyphen, like many hyphens, is more illustrative of anxiety than comradery.[6]

Cohen's intervention is embedded in his title, "The Myth of the Judeo-Christian Tradition" using "tradition" and "myth" to offset the lie that lurks beneath, or inside, the hyphen. Who gets to coin something a "tradition"? Cohen, following Foucault, suggests it is only those in power. After all, it is the Christian and *not* the Jew who *invents* the Judeo-Christian tradition. The Jew may support the Judeo-Christian tradition for the purposes of power or influence but there is nothing *intrinsic* to Judaism that would need a Judeo-Christian tradition at all. Thus Cohen writes, "We can learn much from the history of Jewish-Christian relations, but the one thing we cannot make of it is a discourse of community, fellowship, and understanding. How then, can we make of it a tradition?"[7] By juxtaposing "tradition" and "myth" in the title, Cohen seeks to mine the origins of this move by Christian America. Why Jews, why "Judeo," why forge a "tradition" with the very people whose rejection stands at the center of your covenant? And what then is the price or benefit of all this in a secular society, a secular "tradition" that has no history, perhaps invented only to fortify exceptionalism?

Cohen argues that this "Judeo-Christian tradition" is not a gesture of reconciliation at all but rather the consummation of absorption whereby the "Jew," now Latinized/Christianized as "Judeo," becomes fully a part of Christian America. For Cohen it is a cynical act of assimilation and the erasure of significant difference. Why then do American Jews buy in? Here Cohen sees this "myth" as a product of disaster and not triumph: It is the disaster of faith now lost and the triumphal substitute of secular religiosity. He writes, "Such secular religiosity is dangerous; it is the common quicksand of Jews and Christians."[8] Elsewhere Samuel Belkin, a leader of American Orthodoxy in mid-century wrote, "The greatest danger . . . to traditional Judaism lies in the philosophy of secular observance."[9] Belkin was likely referring to non-Orthodox observance, but his comment resonates with Cohen; when secularism becomes the lens through which religion is refracted and in Belkin's case, enacted, certain dangers emerge. For Belkin the danger may be the loss of authenticity; for Cohen it may be the erasure of the Jew. What is at stake for us, Jews and Americans, when this double exceptionalism becomes operative?

The "myth" in Cohen's mind serves the failure of each against the other and then both against a common enemy (the non "Judeo-Christian"). "The Christian comes to depend on the Jew for an explanation of unredeemedness. The Jew . . . must look to Christianity to ransom for him his faith in the Messiah, to renew for him his expectation of the nameless Christ."[10] This is reminiscent of an older idea attributed to the neo-Kantian philosopher Hermann Cohen that false messiahs are necessary as they keep the messianic idea alive. Arthur Cohen suggests the Jew and Christian use one another, must use one another, to satisfy the lack in both. But they use one another at their own peril. For Arthur Cohen the price for the Jew may be too high and the benefit is too meager. But something more pernicious may be going on in this new (Christian) gesture to the Jews. Santiago Slabodsky writes about how some theorists have suggested that the existence of this newfangled Judeo-Christian project sets conditions for yet another possible atrocity.

Indeed in recent decades several scholars have pointed to the existence of a 'new ecumenical deal' in religious and political secular forms that enables Western Christianity to expiate her sins incurred from her ideological and material complicity (or leadership) during the Holocaust. The outcome of this new Judeo-Christian project, dissident voices argue, goes even further than ethno-religious exculpation. It has enabled the West to perpetuate the same civilization atrocities by, ironically, justifying their reproduction with the excuse of protecting its former victims. In this way Jews became re-inscribed into the same dualistic paradigm that was responsible for the annihilation of one-third of their population during World War II.[11]

While the prediction may seem overly dramatic, the point is well-taken: the enemy becomes the friend to perpetrate new acts of oppression on a common enemy (the non Judeo-Christian). Have Jews been drawn into a secular orbit of power that threatens the religious tradition upon which their identity is based? What of Judaism has been abandoned to be part of the Judeo-Christian tradition?

For Cohen this theo-political expression of exceptionalism all illustrates the death of religion, both Judaism and Christianity. If Jews and Christians should find their footing inside "tradition," he argues, each would dismiss the "myth" as unnecessary and could (happily) return to seeing the irreconcilability of one to the other. In short, for Cohen, irreconcilability is lost when each religion "loses its religion." That is, if each had their tradition, there would no longer be a need for a Judeo-Christian tradition. If they do not, and the myth persists as "masking the abyss," of the Judeo-Christian tradition, it will be the catalyst for the disappearance of both, which means, I think, that only Christianity remains, albeit an imperialistic shell of itself. The "myth" is constructed from the shards of each "tradition" shell-shocked by modernity's critique. What gets saved is only power and what gets lost is the (prophetic) critique of power in both religions. Cohen, of course, cares for the Jews here above all—can the Jews survive in a tolerant society, even one that wants to embrace them through a Judeo-Christian tradition? His answer is only if it resists the embrace, because the embrace is self-serving of a Christianity that "can no longer deal with actual history."[12] The Jew then becomes the consolation of history.

The Christian erasure of the Jew for the sake of the common enemy comes through quite starkly in Steve Bannon's talk at a 2014 symposium at the Vatican where he laid out his worldview.[13] In his expansive remarks lasting almost an hour, Bannon consistently referred to the "Judeo-Christian West" but whenever he defined it, he always reverted to exclusively Christian language, such as "the church militant," "the underlying spiritual and moral foundations of Christianity," a time when "Christian faith was predominant throughout [a] Europe of practicing Christians." The only place where he mentions Judaism is in reference to capitalists who, he says, "were either active particpants in the Jewish faith, [or] active participants in the Christians' faith, . . . and they took their beliefs . . . in the work they did." This is, of course, empirically false at least in regards to Jews and capitalism. Many Jewish capitalists in Western Europe were quite assimilated and many, especially in Eastern Europe, who had strong ties to religion were sympathetic to socialism. In any case, in some way agreeing with Cohen, Bannon says, "I certainly think secularism has sapped the strength of the Judeo-Christian West to defend its ideals." Yet what Bannon wants to do is re-insert "religion" as the theological foundation of a secular exercise in power against the true enemy: Islam. For Bannon it is the Judeo-Christian tradition that serves as the exceptionalist fuel to engage in a war against Islam, dragging the Jews into a modern-day Christian crusade.

Where Bannon shows what he means by the "Judeo-Christian West" comes out twice in his remarks. First, defining it against "a barbaric empire in the Far East," and second, "the long history of the Judeo-Christian West's struggle against Islam." To the second point, Jews never had a "struggle against Islam," at least not until the advent of Zionism. There was certainly oppression and persecution but the notion of a "struggle against Islam" is not endemic to the Judaic tradition. In fact, arguably without Islam the entire medieval Jewish philosophical tradition would not exist. It was through Arabic translations of Plato and Aristotle in the ninth century that Jews were exposed to the Greek philosophical corpus. And more practically, Jews generally lived better under Muslim rule than they did in Christendom, which persecuted, tortured, and murdered them for centuries. Not very "Judeo-Christian." Bannon here proves my claim that Judeo-Christian is really an iteration of secular Christian exceptionalism, a position that can perhaps include present-day Israel because it, too, struggles against Islam. In his 2007 book *A Match Made in Heaven*, Zev Chafetz aptly calls this situation a "Judeo-Evangelical Alliance."[14] But in reality there is no "Judeo-Christian West"; there is the Christian West and the myth of a Judeo-Christian tradition.

But perhaps what this is really about, for the Jew and for the Christian, and certainly for Bannon and his supporters, is the reiteration of the exceptionalism of both through the prism of the other. That which both were historically prohibited from doing with the other emerges in the hyphen that brings them together. Cohen's essay was written decades before the rise of Islamism and Islamophobia and before the Israeli occupation (it was written only two years after the Six-Day War). What can Cohen say to us about the Jew today, construed, or re-invented as "Judeo," at this time when American exceptionalism has both become government policy in Donald Trump's "America First" campaign (an inversion of American imperialism that amounts to same thing) as well as a religious mandate in a theopolitical register through the rise of evangelical political piety? Has Cohen's godless communism today become Radical Islam? Has the secular

Cold War morphed into a resacralized crusade giving white nationalists like Richard Spencer, Steve Bannon, and the alt right, new voices on the American landscape?

As I read Cohen, there is a double exceptionalism going on in the Judeo-Christian. Cohen argues that the Judeo-Christian tradition is really a tool of domination in regards to Judaism and Jews. I add that it also invites the Jew to have a hand in wielding the hammer of power against the non–Judeo-Christian. It invites the Jew to join American exceptionalism by re-framing her own exceptionalism in the service of America. By subsuming the "Judeo" in the Christian, Christianity owns its "Judeo" roots and thus takes from the Jew that which she always used as the firewall between Judaism and its perceived theological foe. In this case, tolerance is the mask of domination. As I have argued elsewhere, President Trump's unilateral decision to move the US Embassy to Jerusalem, taking the vexing issue of Jerusalem off the table as a precondition of negotiations, is not only a victory for Israel but also a victory for America (and thus Christianity).[15] Jerusalem may be Israel's capital, but America is really the sovereign. For the Jew the price of joining its exceptionalism with America is high indeed.

The state of Israel and the role it plays in American Judeo-Christian exceptionalism is something Cohen never addressed. Recently in America, the "Judeo" does not only mean the "Jew" but also the "Jew/ish" nation-state. In this sense, Judeo-Christian is part of a larger Zionist narrative expressed by today's American politicians, who proudly proclaim that "there is no light between the US and Israel" and who unilaterally decide who "owns" Jerusalem. Even the hyphen collapses. This benefits the "Jew" as "Israel" in precisely the same way it threatens the "Jew" as "American." The theo-political "Judeo-Christian" is a tool of exceptionalism to the non "Judeo-Christian," the Muslim "other," the Palestinian, the enemy (non-Zionists?). The historical pact between Jews and Muslims that is in many ways crucial for Israel's long-term survival has been subverted such that the Christian now becomes the political ally of the Jew against the Muslim through the "Judeo-Christian" expressed, in part, through American fidelity to Israel. Israel, as the "Judeo" becomes an appendage of American exceptionalism.

With Cohen, but for different reasons, I think this merging exceptionalism is a dangerous game. First, as Slobodsky suggested above it offers a new theo-political exceptionalism that may seem more palatable because it includes the "Judeo" and thus gestures toward enlightened progress. "We will no longer seek to convert you, we will now include you," but this inclusion comes at a price: you are now part of *our* exceptionalism. This itself is a kind of exclusion, not only of the Jew who is distinct from the "Judeo" (perhaps the Jew who is critical of Israel?) but for the non-Judeo-Christian in America as well. But as a myth, of course, it only "masks the abyss" here until the moment when it is no longer necessary.

Second, the new "Judeo-Christian" severs, or at the very least complicates, ties between Jew and Muslim, making the former now a party to the latter's complex history of the latter. In this sense, the Judeo-Christian makes the Jew a pseudo-Christian in the Christian-Muslim narrative of theo-political power. So now it is the Zionist Jew who becomes the "Judeo" in the Judeo-Christian. Many Israeli leaders readily, and cynically, court Christian Zionists knowing that their endgame is very different. But that support has its price. The freedom such collusion offers may very well be the servitude of the "Judeo" (perhaps even Israel) to the Christian (America) if and when things change.

Cohen was afraid for the American Jew. He viewed the American Judeo-Christian tradition as a veil for the *erasure* of Judaism at the price of the *survival* of the Jew. And in 1969 talk of Jewish survival was a growing concern, not as much because of anti-Semitism but because of assimilation.[16] The Judeo-Christian myth for Cohen was one form of that assimilation in the guise of a pact of shared exceptionalism. Post 9/11 things are of a different order. Today the exceptionalist implications are more global, certainly for (Christian) America and even for the (Judeo) Jew. I think this was the underlying premise of Bannon's remarks. Each (Jew and Christian) can now more readily than in 1969 use the other for its own exceptionalist purposes: the Jew by saying that finally Christians have understood that without Judaism Christianity cannot survive theologically, and Christianity by saying that we can subsume the Jew through assimilation with the mere inclusion of the prefix "Judeo." Each gets something from the bargain. The Zionist Jew gets America to support its exceptionalist claims. And Christianity gets to feel exonerated by now including the Jew, whom it very recently tried to destroy, into its orbit of power and dominance. And both Jew (Zionists and Israel) and Christian (imperialist America) can use the Judeo-Christian to justify its claim to exclusive right (and perhaps even divine right) to pursue its intended goals, even as the Judeo-Christian may make those goals impossible to achieve.

Notes

1. Jerome Gellman, "Jewish Chosenness and Religious Diversity—A Contemporary Approach," in *Religious Perspectives on Religious Diversity*, ed. Robert McKim (Leiden: Brill, 2016), 23.

2. Interestingly, militant rabbi Meir Kahane, responding to the Israeli Parliament claiming he was a racist, argued that secular Zionists and secular Jews in general, that is, those for

whom Zionism or Jewish election is not founded exclusively on divine revelation, are "racists." "This is why the religious Jew must raise his voice night and day against the continued specter of racism that is the very essence of the secular Jew." Meir Kahane, "I Hate Racism" (1987), in Rabbi Meir Kahane, *Beyond Words: Selected Writings 1960–1990*, vol. 5 (Jerusalem: Institute for Publication of the Writings of Rabbi Meir Kahane, 2010), 226. In his *Judaism and Zionism: A New Theory*, David Novak makes a similar, albeit not as sharp, accusation regarding secular Jewish claims to the land of Israel. See David Novak, *Judaism and Zionism: A New Theory* (Cambridge, UK: Cambridge University Press), 2, 3, 71, 144, and also Shaul Magid, "Politics and Precedent: David Novak, Meir Kahane, and Yoel Teitelbaum (the Satmar Rebbe) on *Judaism and Zionism*," in *Covenantal Thinking: Essays on the Philosophy of David Novak* (Toronto: University of Toronto Press, forthcoming).

3. Alan Brinkley, *American History, A Survey*, vol. 2, 9th ed. (New York: McGraw-Hill, 1995), 352.

4. On the history of the term, especially in America, see Mark Silk, "Notes on the Judeo-Christian Tradition in America," *American Quarterly* 36, no. 1 (Spring 1984): 65–85.

5. See Arthur Cohen, "The Myth of the Judeo-Christian Tradition," *Commentary Magazine*, November 1, 1969, https://www.commentarymagazine.com/articles/the-myth-of-the-judeo-christian-tradition/. The essay also appeared as the title essay of Cohen's *The Myth of the Judeo-Christian Tradition* (New York: Schoken Books, 1971). Page numbers refer to the *Commentary Magazine* article. For a similar critique of the Judeo-Christian myth published in *The Jewish Liberation Journal*, November, 1970, see Aviva Cantor Zukoff, "The Oppression of America's Jews," re-printed in *Jewish Radicalism*, ed. Jack Nusan Porter and Peter Dreier (New York: Grove Press, 1973), 42, 43.

6. See Berel Lang, "Hyphenated Jews and the Anxiety of Identity," *Jewish Social Studies* 12, no. 1 (Autumn, 2005): 1–15 and Jonathan Sarna, "The Cult of Synthesis in American Jewish Culture," *Jewish Social Studies* 5, nos. 1, 2 (Autumn 1998–Winter 1999): 52–79.

7. Cohen, "The Myth," 74.

8. Cohen, "The Myth," 77.

9. Belkin, *Essays in Traditional Jewish Thought* (New York: Philosophical Library, 1956), 38.

10. Cohen, "The Myth," 77.

11. Santiago Slabodsky, *Decolonial Judaism: Triumphal Failures of Barbaric Thinking* (New York: Palgrave, 2014), 6, 7.

12. Cohen, "The Myth," 77.

13. See J. Lester Feder, "This is How Steve Bannon Sees the Entire World," *Buzzfeed*, November 15, 2016, https://www.buzzfeed.com/lesterfeder/this-is-how-steve-bannon-sees-the-entire-world?utm_term=.xqWMeyVV9#.ho8NaOrrx; cf. Hannah Roberts, "Steve Bannon's Alt-right academy—And One Village's Fight to Stop It," *FT Magazine*, https://www.ft.com/content/d38ffde2-6bf6-11e9-a9a5-351eeaef6d84.

14. Zev Chafetz, *A Match Made in Heaven: American Jews, Christian Zionists, and One Man's Exploration of the Weird and Wonderful Judeo-Evangelical Alliance* (New York: Harper Collins, 2009).

15. See Shaul Magid, "Gold-Plated Jerusalem," *Contending Modernities*, December 14, 2017, http://contendingmodernities.nd.edu/global-currents/gold-plated-jerusalem/.

16. See Jonathan Woocher, *Sacred Survival: The Civil Religion of American Jews* (Bloomington: Indiana University Press, 1986).

14

Sacrifice

Stephanie Frank

IT HAS BEEN FREQUENTLY REMARKED THAT CARL SCHMITT'S OEU-vre has, to a great extent, molded contemporary conversations around "political theology." All of the concepts of modern political theory, Schmitt advances, are structurally analogous to theological concepts (God, the miracle, etc.): thus, "political theology" names a political theory that is analogical to a particular sort of theology. In Schmitt's framework, political theology is fundamentally about the question of sovereignty, and sovereignty is founded on the exception, or the suspension of law.

But there are other ways of understanding political theology. Particularly in the American context, there has been discussion of political theology as linked to a theology of providence: the United States has some sort of divinely elected role to play in the unfolding of history. Many of the most vivid recent evocations of this theology came in the first years of the new millennium, and particularly from George W. Bush, in the context of the justification of US military interventions in Iraq and Afghanistan. For instance, Bush said the following in his 2003 State of the Union address:

> [W]e go forward with confidence, because this call of history has come to the right country. . . . America is a strong nation and honorable in the use of our strength. We exercise power without conquest, and we sacrifice for the liberty of strangers.
>
> Americans are a free people who know that freedom is the right of every person and the future of every nation. The liberty we prize is not America's gift to the world; it is God's gift to humanity.
>
> We Americans have faith in ourselves, but not in ourselves alone. We do not know—we do not claim to know all the ways of providence, yet we can trust in them, placing our confidence in the loving God behind all of life and all of history.[1]

As my colleague Shaul Magid notes in this volume, this construction of American exceptionalism draws on the precedent of Jewish exceptionalism, with its notion of divine election—right down to the peculiar linking of divine election with entitlement to land. Of course, even in current American political discourse, one still encounters the echoes of the doctrine of Manifest Destiny—particularly in the context of debates about, for instance, federal initiatives that impact Indian reservations.

Paul Kahn's book *Political Theology: Four New Chapters on the Concept of Sovereignty*—as the title implies, a kind of reimagining of Schmitt's work—takes on the project of delineating a phenomenology of the American political imaginary.[2] That is, Kahn wants to offer an account of the contours of the conceptual landscape that constitutes Americans' ideas about their own politics.[3] To do so, he explicitly thematizes a different kind of political theology. Kahn's political theology frames sacrifice as a (perhaps *the*) central question of the field. (This marks one of the ways in which Kahn departs from Schmitt, though it is not clear that he understands this.)[4] Though there are many aspects of Kahn's argument with which I disagree, I think Kahn is right to direct our attention to the notion of sacrifice, which has received significantly less attention in the discourse on political theology than either sovereignty or providence. In this piece I want to take up the question of the political theology of sacrifice with regard to American exceptionalism.

Though—as you will see in the excerpt that follows—Kahn directly engages the issue of American exceptionalism, he does not approach it immediately from his central problematic of sacrifice. Rather, he links Schmitt's notion of the exception (the declaration of which is the constitutive mark of the sovereign) to exceptionalism. Schmitt considered that there was something quasi-theological about the deciding of the exception, which is to say, the suspension of the constitutional order; for Kahn, that decision is *actually* theological, or, as he sometimes prefers, "sacred."[5]

Kahn's text is predicated on a distinction between the political imaginary of liberalism, which (on his analysis) denies that there is an outside to the rule of law—in his view, this political comportment is apotheosized in the European Union—and theological political imaginaries, which, like that of the United States, keep alive the possibility of the "exception," or the suspension of the rule of law. What Kahn finds interesting about the US case is that the American notion of popular sovereignty "links the Constitution—and thus the rule of law—to the Revolution; it links law to exception" (10).

By this, Kahn seems to intend to say that the US political imaginary is shaped by the fact that the Constitution is explicitly conceptualized as a kind of irruption of popular sovereignty: it codifies the "decision" taken to break with the British. Thus (according to Kahn) the very fact of the rule of law, in the US case, always rearticulates the possibility of its suspension: the US constitution is unique (and America 'exceptional') insofar as it preserves the imaginability of unconstrained sovereignty.[6] (Kahn does not mention the parallel, but this claim itself evokes a tradition of Christian exceptionalism: in Christianity, the eternal enters into the historical; in the US, the exception enters into the legal order.)

What is unclear, here, is why exactly Kahn imagines the United States to be a special case. Its opacity notwithstanding, Kahn's argument takes the form that it is something about the US Constitution (or the circumstances of the codification of the US Constitution) that gives us the constellation of attitudes distinctive to American exceptionalism. He links this (again, obscurely) to violence, suggesting that the social contract converts murder into sacrifice. But presumably Kahn does not think the US Constitution is somehow different than other constitutions in its origins in a "decision": every constitution involves a suspension of the previous order. And of course the United States is neither the first nor the last constitutional discourse to include significant discussion of the right of revolution—which is the most important way that the notion of the decision-making power of the popular sovereign is enshrined in law.

It is hard, then, to imagine how it could be argued that the US Constitution is in its substance different than other constitutions in this regard. But Kahn is interested in American exceptionalism. So I think Kahn's position must be that the United States' *imagination* of its Constitution more prominently features the "right of revolution" than other political imaginaries: the idea of the legal order is intertwined with the idea of the exception in the way that Americans think about politics.

I am not sure this is correct—indeed, I'm not even sure exactly how we would go about deciding if this were correct. In what follows, I suggest that Kahn's idea of a political theology of sacrifice might be brought to bear to illuminate American exceptionalism. Kahn does gesture toward a connection between his emphasis on sacrifice and his ruminations on American exceptionalism as related to the exception's imbrication in the Constitution. Though his argument on this point is not totally clear, it appears that he wants to draw a connection between the instituting violence of the American Revolution and the power of the rhetoric of sacrifice in contemporary US political discourse. He writes, "Political violence has always been and remains a form of sacrifice. . . . Moreover, the moment at which such sacrifice is performed is always that of the exception" (7).

This claim is problematic on multiple levels. First, Kahn does not distinguish between various types of political violence in his clamor to think about the US political imaginary as deeply sacrificial. But clearly the American heroization of those who are willing to sacrifice themselves in its defense is distinguishable from frequent moves to mark certain people as enemies—and worthy targets of violence for that reason.[7]

Moreover, since Agamben's *Homo Sacer*—also inspired, in part, by Schmitt's political theology—*homo sacer* is the exception, the man "outside the law" (*sacer* means, originally, "set apart") precisely *because* he cannot be sacrificed. That is, the scope of sacrifice defines the scope of the community and the rule of law.[8] Regardless of Kahn's peculiar (and unsubstantiated) interpretation of sacrifice as always summoning forth a moment of exception, I am dubious that his construction of political violence in the framework of exception provides resources for understanding American exceptionalism or its particular character. After all, the United States is hardly the only country to have had a violent revolution ending in a new constitution. In fact, Kahn makes, in his text, only vague gestures toward what the American Revolution actually entailed. I think, ultimately, that this vagueness highlights an important truth: the "decision" of the Revolution notwithstanding, violence does not feature so strongly in the American political imaginary as the trace of its war for colonial independence.

Nevertheless, I think Kahn is right to suggest that sacrifice looms distinctively large in the American political imaginary. Just the last few years provide several moments in public discourse where this was readily apparent. Consider, for instance, Khizr Khan's speech at the Democratic National Convention in 2016. Standing next to his wife, Khan—an immigrant—waved his copy of the Constitution in the context of his invocation of his son's sacrifice. He asked Donald Trump whether he had read the Constitution and reminded him of those momentous words of the Fourteenth Amendment, "equal protection of the law." He asked, "*Have you ever been to Arlington Cemetery? Go look at the graves of brave patriots who died defending the United States of America. You will see all faiths, genders, and ethnicities.*" Pointedly, he remarked to an absent Trump, "*You have sacrificed nothing and no one.*" Clearly, contextually, Khan's ground to speak was afforded him by his son's death—and he used his platform to scold a politician widely seen as not having made any "sacrifices" (whether in the form of personal suffering, dead children, or taxes paid).

Or consider the controversy about the football player Colin Kaepernick's refusal to stand for the national anthem. One common refrain was that his action was "disrespectful to the military." The idea that acts of protest engaging national symbols are particularly offensive to the military would seem to get backwards the relationship between the nation and its defense. But if it is a confusion, it is an extraordinarily widespread confusion, which of course tends to suggest that it is not a confusion at all. Kahn's argument gestures in the direction that the reflexive association of national symbols with members of the military follows from the contours of American political theology. Members of the military stand in a privileged relationship to the idea of the nation because of their proximity to sacrifice.

I wonder if we might assemble the pieces to this puzzle (American exceptionalism, sacrality, and violence) in a different way if we were to more precisely theorize sacrifice. Almost every intellectual lineage of the study of religion draws lines that connect through the dot of Marcel Mauss and Henri Hubert's 1899 *Sacrifice: Its Nature and Function*.[9] This seminal text suggested that sacrifice was not about appeasing gods or communing with gods (the major theories before this contribution) but rather about creating gods who could be appeased or with whom one could commune. In other words, sacrifice (*sacer* + *facere*) is literally about making the sacred, about generating sacrality. We create the idea of entities worth sacrificing for precisely by sacrificing for them.

What, though, would be (or would be thought to be) distinctively American about this dynamic? What could this have to do with American exceptionalism? I wonder if the prominence of sacrifice is the flipside of America's (perhaps not entirely honest) emphasis on the uniqueness of its own past vis-à-vis the issue of secularism. It has often (too often?) been said that one of the distinctive features of the United States is its pastlessness, or again, the fact that it was born modern. We are (the line runs, disingenuously) a country for whom church and state were distinguished from the beginning. A corollary of this imaginary underscores the absence of the old gods and their traces. (Indeed, the parallel situation of the twilight of the old gods in Third Republic France is, I have argued elsewhere, a major contributor to the genesis of the project that Mauss and Hubert began with *Sacrifice: Its Nature and Function*, which eventually gave rise to the theory of religion of their collaborator, Mauss' uncle, Emile Durkheim.)[10] Perhaps America's obsessive statement and restatement of its lack of old gods—its lack of a history of church interference in the public sphere—inspires an anxiety that causes our preoccupation with the creation of new ones through sacrifice.

When we conjoin Hubert and Mauss's theory of sacrifice with Durkheim's theory of religion and Agamben's reflections on the figure of *homo sacer*, we can see that by choosing which deaths to deem sacrificial, the collective is simultaneously constructing a version of itself to venerate. We discuss this question, after a fashion, when we discuss police "murders" of unarmed people of color in the US as opposed to when we discuss the "sacrifice" of police officers. We discuss it when we discuss drone killings of US citizens who are suspected terrorists and when we discuss accidental civilian casualties. We also discuss it, to return to Magid, when we discuss the way the Israeli state ought to construct its Palestinian citizens.

If Agamben would figure us all as either potential victims of sacrifice or potential victims of murder, recent realities (both in the US and elsewhere) make clear that people are dying and dying violently who are (by Agamben's lights) neither sacrificeable nor (by the lights of the collective) murderable. Not coincidentally, particularly in the wake of the rash of school shootings of the last two decades, we have begun to see there is a new discourse about sacrifice to false gods. Or rather—false gods being created by wrong sacrifices. Some have figured the deaths of the victims of the Parkland shooting as sacrifices on the altar of the Second Amendment. Others, more darkly still, have figured the deaths as sacrifices to Moloch, recalling the famous words of Milton.

> First MOLOCH, horrid King besmear'd with blood
> Of human sacrifice, and parents tears,
> Though, for the noyse of Drums and Timbrels loud,
> Their children's cries unheard that passed through fire
> To his grim Idol. Him the AMMONITE
> Worshipt in RABBA and her watry Plain,
> In ARGOB and in BASAN, to the stream
> Of utmost ARNON. Nor content with such
> Audacious neighbourhood, the wisest heart
> Of SOLOMON he led by fraud to build
> His Temple right against the Temple of God
> On that opprobrious Hill, and made his Grove
> The pleasant Vally of HINNOM, TOPHET thence
> And black GEHENNA call'd, the Type of Hell.[11]

Those who sacrificed to Moloch were not only vilified for the grisly nature of their sacrificial victims, but also for sacrificing to a false god; indeed, as the passage from Milton makes clear, the grisly nature of their sacrifice is conceived as bound up with their worship of a false God. And if we take the purpose of sacrifice to be making sacred, as I have suggested we should, these deaths are problematic: the bounds of the sacrificial ritual no longer coincide with the bounds of the social contract. The thing that is being endowed with sacrality is wrongly sanctified. Does the sketch of the American imaginary in terms of "political theology" open the question of an American political idolatry?

Notes

1. George W. Bush, "State of the Union Address," January 28, 2003. For more on the political theology of providence that characterized George W. Bush's presidency, see Bruce Lincoln, "Bush's God-Talk," in *Political Theologies: Public Religions in a Post-Secular World*, ed. Hent de Vries and Lawrence Sullivan (New York: Fordham University Press, 2006).

2. Paul W. Kahn, *Political Theology: Four New Chapters on the Concept of Sovereignty* (New York: Columbia University Press, 2011).

3. Kahn frames his text as answering the question of "What do we learn if we engage Schmitt's argument from a perspective that substitutes the popular sovereign for his idea of the sovereign?" (9) But Lars Vinx has (correctly) noted that though Kahn imagines that he is, here, breaking new ground, Schmitt quite clearly makes room for—and even explicitly considers—the possibility that the sovereign might be "the people." Lars Vinx, review of *Political Theology: Four New Chapters on the Concept of Sovereignty* by Paul Kahn, *Notre Dame Philosophical Reviews*, June 22, 2011, https://ndpr.nd.edu/reviews/political-theology-four-new -chapters-on-the-concept-of-sovereignty/.

4. As John Wolfe Ackerman notes, "Whereas Schmitt insists (questionably) that politics only exists where the extreme possibility of violent death in war also exists (as the most extreme form of political conflict), Kahn maintains that politics is, most fundamentally and in its very grammar, such violence." John Wolfe Ackerman, "Why Political Theology Again?," review of Paul W. Kahn, *Political Theology: Four New Chapters on the Concept of Sovereignty* and *Sacred Violence: Torture, Terror, and Sovereignty*," *Tulsa Law Review* 48, no. 2 (2012): https://www.libraryofsocialscience.com/assets/pdf/Ackerman-Why_Political_T.pdf.

5. Kahn uses "sacred" and "theological" interchangeably, for reasons that are unclear to me (and which probably relate to his failure to theorize sacrifice).

6. For Kahn, this manifests in a variety of ways. For instance, on his analysis, the American doctrine of judicial review is an exemplification: the Supreme Court rules in the name of the Constitution, which is essentially to say, in the name of a transhistorical political sovereign that supersedes the result of legislative process. Similarly, presidents have (particularly recently) rejected the War Powers Act, preserving for themselves the ultimate "deciding power" when it comes to matters of war and peace.

7. As Kahn himself writes, "American history begins with the Revolution and continues today in the war on terror" (16).

8. Kahn gives a nod to Agamben's position, or something like it, when he suggests that the social contract converts murder into sacrifice.

9. Henri Hubert and Marcel Mauss, *Sacrifice: Its Nature and Function*, trans W.D. Halls (Chicago: University of Chicago Press, 1964).

10. For an alternative strand of the relationship of Mauss and Hubert's theory of sacrifice to its historical context—in particular *l'affaire Dreyfus*—see Ivan Strenski, *Contesting Sacrifice* (Chicago: University of Chicago Press, 2002).

11. Milton, *Paradise Lost*, 1.392–405.

15

Two Theologies of Chosenness

Benjamin L. Berger

WHAT MUST WE EXPLAIN IF WE ARE SEEKING TO UNDERSTAND THE
theologies of US exceptionalism? One answer is that our burden is to explain the particular. Here, the appropriate move is to examine the unique
histories and imaginative formations of religious, legal, and political life
in the United States. We might look to the unique religious history of the
early colonies, to the distinctive role that "Church" plays in US constitutional life, or to the tethering of the market, politics, and religion that has
a particular shape and force in US political and legal life. With this move,
one is seeking to identify the features that generate a theological-political
configuration peculiar to the United States. On this approach, an inquiry
into exceptionalism is an inquiry into difference: it is an effort to identify
the features that make US political life and self-understanding unique or
distinctive from those of other political communities. The specific—and
deeply interesting—question of the theologies of US exceptionalism is a
question of the role that particular understandings of, and relationships to,
religion and the sacred play in constituting that unique political identity.
We are here seeking to explain that which makes this community unique;
we are interested in its specificity.

This inquiry into the particular is the character of Paul Kahn's project in *Political Theology: Four New Chapters on the Concept of Sovereignty,*
the book that is the focus of Stephanie Frank's contribution to this volume.[1] Interested in mapping the structure, beliefs, and meaning that shape
the American political and legal imagination, Kahn maps the distinctive

constellation of revolution, sacrifice, and popular sovereignty that, for him, shape this political identity. In his examination of popular sovereignty, violence, and sacred meaning, Kahn is seeking to describe that which makes this political community understand itself as a uniquely compelling candidate for love and sacrifice. A particular American relationship to revolution and constitution sits at the heart of his account in this and his other work.[2] As a non-American, Kahn's account indeed seems to capture features distinctive to the American political imaginary. But Frank levies an interesting objection. Don't all constitutions have their origin in a decision, she asks, and aren't violence and sovereignty at work in the construction of all political communities? And so she seeks to "assemble the pieces to this puzzle" somewhat differently, arguing that it is instead the peculiar salience of the friend-enemy distinction, not the decision, that distinguishes the phenomenology of US politics and the "violence directed against the enemy, which endows the political commitments of 'Americanness' with sacrality."[3]

But with both her critique and her alternative, Frank gestures towards a difficulty with focusing on the particular when seeking to explain the puzzles—theological and otherwise—involved in "US exceptionalism." Every constitution is distinctive, the particular expression of a political and historical self-understanding. Every constitution is someone's constitution. The moment it ceases to be so—the moment a constitution ceases to be specifically "ours"—it ceases to discharge its constituting function. This is true of law more generally: its authority flows from the belief that this is, in an important sense, "my law." In this respect, although American political history and the culture of law's rule in the United States may generate distinctive contours, some vision of popular sovereignty is essential to our ideas of modern law. Frank's proposed focus on the dynamics of sacrality involved in the friend-enemy distinction replicates the issue: for Schmitt the friend-enemy distinction is not an occasional feature of some politics. Rather, it is definitional of the political.[4] We might be able to describe the particular ways in which the distinction is deployed in the US—or even its particular fierceness or salience—but we ought to expect to find it at work wherever we find the political. And, of course, every political community has a unique historical and contemporary relationship with religion and place for religion in the political; as Talal Asad put it, in matters of religion, "[a]ll modern states . . . are built on complicated emotional inheritances."[5] The point is that a focus on the particular gives us rich access to understanding better what is unique about a particular theological-political formation, but this particularity is something that we all share. It does not get us to the heart of what is intriguing about US exceptionalism. Every community, every constitution, every theology is, in some important respect, particular.

Writing as a Canadian, the puzzle for understanding US exceptionalism is explaining what transforms American particularity into a warrant to exempt or insulate one's legal and political practices from the norms and practices of other communities, or to advance those beliefs at the expense of others. Within the world of legal scholarship, with which I am most familiar, US exceptionalism is associated with practices like the notable non-engagement with comparative and foreign law by US courts[6] and an attitude towards international criminal and human rights law that can lie somewhere between indifference and hostility. Political scientists, experts in international relations, and those more familiar with domestic policy will be better placed to provide examples from their own arenas. But the crux of US exceptionalism, it seems to me, is not simply the existence of distinctive characteristics of an American political way of life, but engagement in practices predicated on the normative priority of that way of life. A description of particularity cannot, on its own, account for US exceptionalism, understood in this way. Indeed, an internalized sense of particularity alone can just as readily lead to an ethic of reciprocity, collaboration, and humility if it inspires a sense of the value, but contingency, of one's own way of being.

And so it is not an appreciation for the fact of particularity *per se* that gets us closer to an understanding of US exceptionalism. Rather, it is understanding the conviction that the particular expresses something of higher, not just unique, truth and appeal. It is only when the particular is projected into that universal register that other norms and meanings appear not only as "other," but as idolatrous, dangerous, or (at minimum) false, thereby authorizing the kinds of practices and postures we associate with exceptionalism. Our burden is explaining how the particular becomes universal. With this as one's focus, the necessary move is, more precisely, to examine the histories, ideas, and structures of belief and practice that might illuminate this translation of the particular into the universal—a universal that has the confidence to traverse other particularities.[7] Perhaps this is what we must explain if we wish to understand the theologies of US exceptionalism.

I cannot confidently offer such an explanation here, for want of intimacy with the American case and the religious histories that have influenced the American political imaginary. Instead, I want to explore a theological concept that might help us to think about this relationship and movement between the particular and the universal, and its political consequences.

I turn to the idea of chosenness. It is not altogether uncommon to draw parallels between American exceptionalism and the idea of a chosen people, familiar in its central theological place within Judaism. In their contributions to this volume, both Frank and Magid make reference to the ways in which American exceptionalism draws in some ways on Jewish chosenness or election. There is no doubt that there is such a "drawing on," but in thinking through American exceptionalism it is edifying and, I suggest, important to explore a distinction between the theological structures of two understandings of the nature of "chosenness."

One understanding approaches chosenness as fundamentally tied to covenant. Indeed, on this view, at work in Exodus 19:3–6, chosenness serves as the theological explanation for the covenant. The tie to covenant lends shape and texture to this sense of chosenness. The covenantal context for election brings with it a specificity, even exclusivity, of relationship. There are no free-floating contracts—they are always between parties—and there is a privity of contract here. Chosenness as linked to a historical, specific relationship brings it close to the idea of treaty: partners choose to enter into a relationship with one another, discharging the duties owed by one to the other. This is the sense of chosenness that undergirds the first prayer of the *Amidah*, central to Jewish liturgy, in which we hear an insistence on the particularity of history, people, and party to covenant:

> Blessed are you our lord, our God and God of our ancestors,
> God of Abraham, Isaac, and God of Jacob,
> God of Sarah, Rebecca, God of Rachel, and God of Leah,
> great, mighty, awe-inspiring, transcendent God,
> who acts with kindness and love, and creates all,
> who remembers the loving deeds of our ancestors,
> and who will lovingly bring a redeemer to their children's children for the sake
> of divine honor.[8]

The petition is to a specific God who is reminded of particular history and relationship to a given people.

Another face of this sense of chosenness—one that is insistent on the particular identity of the parties, duties, and relationships—comes from the word used to describe this elected status in the *tanach*: the word used is *s'gullah*, often translated as "treasured."[9] This word has the distinctive sense of property or possession that makes some sense of a theology in which God could be described as "jealous" in relationship with this "chosen" people. In a version of an essay about which I will say more below, French philosopher Henri Atlan observes that there is a sense of adaptation or adjustment in the verbal form of *s'gullah*, such that "one may speak of the chosen-people concept as pointing to a mutual adaptation between a particular people— a tribe of freed slaves whose existence as a people was inaugurated by the experience of liberation—and its god, who was revealed and defined only in that experience of liberation."[10] This sense of match or specific fittedness— of mutual adaptation of one to the other—plants the meaning of chosenness firmly in the soil of the particular.

There is, however, something embarrassing, troubling, and even historically perilous about the specificity and exclusivity involved in this idea of election or chosenness. Indeed, in the wake of the Jewish emancipation over the nineteenth century, it was worry about the particularity and consequent exclusivity of this Jewish understanding of chosenness that led some Reform and Reconstructionist leaders to seek to universalize the doctrine, preferring to speak of the "mission of Israel."

And this form of response gestures to a second understanding of chosenness, one that is tied to vocation, rather than covenant. The chosenness here is of a message, a set of beliefs, and a mission for those who carry them. It resists particularity—chafes on it—and responds with a turn to universality. The relevant community becomes that of any and all believers in this single, chosen truth. There is a theology that supports this understanding of chosenness as well: the sacred is not tribal, tied to a community of particular identity, and "adapted" to a particular people; it is, rather, found in a universal truth available and appropriate for all, and accessible through faith or grace, not identity. This movement from the particular to the universal in the understanding of chosenness and the theology that supports it is, in essence, the Pauline turn that helped to differentiate Christianity from Judaism. It is a gesture of openness and inclusion, but one that puts a different set of political attitudes and relationships in play. Badiou describes this Pauline move as seeking to avoid both the ideological generality of the Greeks and the particularism of the Jews, pursuing a "universal singularity."[11] Here, "[t]ruth is diagonal relative to every communitarian subset; it neither claims authority from, nor (this is obviously the most delicate point) constitutes any identity. It is offered to all, or addressed to everyone, without a condition of belonging being able to limit this offer, or this address."[12] This is a foundation for a very different political theology.

In an intriguing essay titled, "A people they say is elected . . . ,"[13] published in 1982 in *Le genre humain*, French philosopher Henri Atlan seized on this distinction between a particularistic and universalistic conception of a "chosen people." He observed that the translation of chosenness into an individual reality—and thereby potentially universal—offered the promise of "communication among people of different cultures"[14] and that the Rabbis of early Judaism and the Middle Ages, including Maimonides, recognized this. But he explains that in their case the starting point for opening up to an inner and potentially universal discourse was the particular experience of the law and of an identity that was deepened from within. That identity sought to relinquish nothing of its particular humanity, thus achieving rapport with other and true universality by taking differences into account.[15]

Here, election is defined by a particular relation between a given people and their god and intrinsically embedded in an historical and social reality. "By contrast," Atlan claims, "in the two universal monotheistic religions, the election has become that of believers—*individuals*, and the community is defined as believers—by a single God. No longer by a tribal god, nor even by a god who is 'greater than the others,' but by the only one."[16] Most interesting to me is the moment when Atlan turns his attention to the stakes of these alternate ideas of election; it is here that, in 1982, he explored the kinds of practical ethics and politics that might flow from one or the other theology of chosenness:

> Given the irreducible particularism and egocentrism of every individual, of every family, of every nation, how can we facilitate reciprocal relations among individuals, families, and people? . . . Given the reality of human diversity and particularity, it is probably more realistic and humane to manage relations by taking account of that which each individual and family is called upon to do by its own god, who is different from the others, and to put off the unification of the gods until a messianic era that has yet to arrive.[17]

When we turn back to understanding the theologies of US exceptionalism with these two ideas about chosenness in tow, the picture is provocatively complex. The United States seems to participate strongly in dimensions of both. And this has always been so. As Paul Kahn explains in the text that Stephanie Frank explores, in "all revolutions of the modern period, the quality of the sacred was claimed for both the sovereign people and for reason" and the American Revolution "practiced the same double forms of the sacred, worshiping 'self-evident truths' set forth in the name of 'We the People.'"[18] This intersection of the universal and the particular is familiar, Kahn notes, "from the Jews as the chosen people, to Christ as the realization of universal justice in his singular act of sacrifice."[19] To be sure, there is a profound sense of community history, identity, and exclusivity (and, of late, perhaps particularly the latter) at work in American political life. But as I argued early in this reflection, this particularity is a feature of all political communities—it is what makes comparative constitutional analysis such a rich endeavor. What seems distinctive to the United States, what gets us closer to understanding the theologies of US exceptionalism, is the different ethical horizon of its chosenness. It is the universalist sense of chosenness that can align with the projection of US military might, markets and morals around the world. And it is an odious brand of universal singularity that fuels the exceptionalism on display in the episode involving Steve Bannon that Shaul Magid explores. Face-to-face with US exceptionalism, we seem a significant distance away from the idea of chosenness as rooted in reciprocal regard for particularity on which Atlan lands. The US imaginary may well draw from but significantly transform traditional Jewish ideas of a "chosen people" in the process of generating a sense of theological chosenness that can sustain the practices and attitudes that we associate with US exceptionalism.

Shaul Magid's illuminating reading of Arthur Cohen's 1969 essay, "The Myth of the Judeo-Christian Tradition,"[20] offers a framework for organizing the play of these two ideas of chosenness and their relationship to US exceptionalism. Magid explains that Cohen viewed "the Judeo-Christian tradition" as a tool of domination in respect of the Jews; the hyphen was not a gesture of reconciliation or camaraderie, but a means of absorption. Updating Cohen's anxieties for our moment, Magid shows that adhesion to a "Judeo-Christian tradition" is "one way the theo-political-territorial notion of American exceptionalism can also include the Jews," but he insists that we turn our attention to what is erased and who is conscripted (and to what, against whom?) by this theological confection. It seems to me that a key erasure is of the theological distinctions and possibilities—and their political consequences—available within the idea of chosenness. When Magid describes a sense of election tied to land and specific to people "that is now largely expressed through the realm of a political, or perhaps an imperialist, lens," we are traversing the terrain from the chosenness of covenant to that of universal vocation. Rather than a marker of a generative tension between these two ideas of chosenness and the ethics and politics they differently inspire, the hyphen in Judeo-Christian works as an arrow, appealing to the chosenness of relationship and particularity but then effacing it—or absorbing it—in the movement into a universal register. But in moving away from the particular, one also distances oneself from the complex relations of regard and modesty that can be inspired by that view and of the sort that were so appealing to Atlan. And as this happens, perhaps we have another plotline in the story that seeks to explain the beliefs and meanings that shape the theologies of US exceptionalism, an explanation that I have suggested is most likely to be found in the movement from the particular to the universal. Here we also arrive at one of Magid's most urgent and compelling concerns: that Jewish attachment to the "Judeo-Christian" reshapes the relations and even severs the complex historical ties between Jew and Muslim. Exchanging ideas of chosenness to participate in US exceptionalism—"join[ing] American exceptionalism by reframing her own exceptionalism in the service of America," in Magid's felicitous framing—the Jew finds herself in a very different relationship with Islam, now part of "the Christian-Muslim narrative of theo-political power" enabled, I have ventured, by a specific conception of chosenness.

*   *   *

As I have had the pleasure of reading and thinking with these two pieces by Stephanie Frank and Shaul Magid, my thoughts have consistently returned to the scene involving Khizr Khan's speak to the Democratic National Committee during the 2016 US election race, a speech that Frank raises to explore the particular salience of sacrifice in the American political imagination. The speech surely does this, which she so effectively shows. But what stands out to me from that speech is the remarkable moment in which Khan produces a copy of the US Constitution, provoking an emotional eruption from the audience. It is a moment of great drama. And to a Canadian, and a comparative constitutionalist, it is truly exceptional. Something like this—waving a copy of the constitution at this pitched political moment—would simply not happen in Canada; or, if it did, it would fall flat as a piece of drama. In Britain, they would have nothing to waive, except perhaps a collection of statutes and volumes of the All England Law Reports.

I struggle to put words to why this moment is so exceptional, why it captures something so unique to me as an observer. Why is this moment not only possible but so potent—so moving and effective—in the United States, whereas it would seem so inapt, so discordant, elsewhere?

It seems to me that there is something in this moment that reflects a distinctive relationship with law. In Canada, law is about the messy working out, over time, of particular relationships in a given community. Although it is certainly true that Canadians would regard certain rights contained in the constitution as participating in a global consensus about the construction of just societies, the Canadian constitution is avowedly, and fallibly but exquisitely, particular to us. It is adapted to a particular people. All of this is true of the US Constitution as well—I repeat: every constitution is particular. But this shared particularity does not explain this exceptional moment. There is something more at work. In this holding out of the constitution there is an appeal to sacrality, one that exceeds the preciousness that flows from particularity by drawing on a felt proximity between law, truth, and vocation. It is that form of sacrality, it seems to me, that is distinctive. This moment impresses me as reflective of a political relationship to a constitution that is not just "ours" but also "true" (*self-evidently* so) and of a community with a political theology—and, with it, an exceptionalism—shaped by that conviction.

Notes

1. Paul W. Kahn, *Political Theology: Four New Chapters on the Concept of Sovereignty* (New York: Columbia University Press, 2011).

2. See, e.g., Paul W. Kahn, *Putting Liberalism in Its Place* (Princeton: Princeton University Press, 2004); Paul W. Kahn, *The Reign of Law: Marbury v. Madison and the Construction of America* (New Haven: Yale University Press, 1997).

3. My reading of Kahn's work, and his discussion of the friend-enemy distinction in *Political Theology*, leads me to think that he would be sympathetic to Frank's sense of the importance of this distinction in shaping the American political imaginary.

4. Carl Schmitt, *The Concept of the Political*, trans. George Schwab (Chicago: University of Chicago Press, 1996).

5. Talal Asad, "French Secularism and the 'Islamic Veil Affair,'" *The Hedgehog Review* 8 (2003): 102.

6. See, e.g., Ran Hirschl, *Comparative Matters: The Renaissance of Comparative Constitutional Law* (Oxford: Oxford University Press, 2014).

7. For, as Badiou reminds us, "[t]he universal is not the negation of particularity. It is the measured advance across a distance relative to perpetually subsisting particularity." (Alain Badiou, *Saint Paul: The Foundation of Universalism*, trans. Ray Brassier [Stanford: Stanford University Press, 2003], 110.)

8. This version of the prayer, the *Avot v'Imahot*, includes both the patriarchs and matriarchs. Historically, and in more orthodox liturgies, the *Avot* referenced only the patriarchs.

9. *am s'gullah* is the phrase used to describe Israel as "treasured people" in Deuteronomy 7:6; 14:2, and 26:18–19.

10. Henri Atlan, "Chosen People," in *Contemporary Jewish Religious Thought: Original Essays on Critcial Concepts, Movements, and Beliefs*, ed. Arthur A. Cohen and Paul Mendes-Flohr (New York and London: The Free Press, 1987), 55.

11. Badiou, *Saint Paul*, 13–14.

12. Badiou, 14.

13. Henri Atlan, "Un Peuple Qu'on Dit Élu . . . ," *Le Genre Humain* 1, no. 3–4 (1982): 98–126. I have offered translations aided by the English in a condensed version of the essay published as Atlan, "Chosen People."

14. Atlan, "Un Peuple Qu'on Dit Élu . . . ," 117.

15. Atlan, 117.

16. Atlan, 119 (emphasis in original).

17. Atlan, "Chosen People," 58. I have, here, opted for the language found in the condensed version. The original can be found at Atlan, "Un Peuple Qu'on Dit Élu . . . ," 122.

18. Kahn, *Political Theology*, 21.

19. Kahn, 21.

20. Arthur A. Cohen, "The Myth of the Judeo-Christian Tradition," *Commentary Magazine*, November 1, 1969, https://www.commentarymagazine.com/articles/the-myth-of-the-judeo-christian-tradition/.

Contributors

Elisabeth Anker

Libby Anker's research and teaching interests are at the intersection of political theory, critical theory, cultural analysis, and media studies. Professor Anker received her PhD in political theory from University of California, Berkeley, where she also received a Designated Emphasis in film studies. She has held research fellowships at Brown University's Pembroke Center for Teaching and Research on Women and UC Berkeley's Charles Travers Fellowship in Ethics and Politics. Her research has also been supported by multiple faculty grants from the George Washington University.

Benjamin L. Berger

Benjamin Berger is Professor and York Research Chair in Pluralism and Public Law at Osgoode Hall Law School, York University in Toronto. His areas of research and teaching specialization are law and religion, criminal and constitutional law and theory, and the law of evidence. He is author of *Law's Religion: Religious Difference and the Claims of Constitutionalism* (2015) and general editor of the Hart Publishing series Constitutional Systems of the World.

Faisal Devji

Faisal Devji is Professor of Indian History and Fellow of St. Antony's College at the University of Oxford Yale University. He received his PhD in Intellectual History at the University of Chicago, was Junior Fellow at the Harvard Society of Fellows, and taught at Yale and the New School before joining Oxford. He has been Yves Oltramare Chair at the Graduate Institute in Geneva and is an Institute of Public Knowledge Scholar at NYU. Devji is the author of four books, *Landscapes of the Jihad* (2005), *The Terrorist in Search of Humanity* (2009), *The Impossible Indian* (2012) and *Muslim Zion* (2013).

Spencer Dew

Spencer Dew is Visiting Assistant Professor at Kenyon College and instructor in religious studies at Ohio State University. His book, *The Aliites: Race and Law in the Religions of Noble Drew Ali* (2019) provides a window onto religion, race, citizenship, and law in America.

Stephanie Frank

Stephanie Frank is Associate Professor of Instruction in religion and the humanities in the Humanities, History, and Social Sciences Department at Columbia College Chicago. Professor Frank has published extensively on various problematics related to secularization in journals of anthropology, intellectual history, political science, and religious studies. Her current project is a book considering the methodological divergences between Durkheim and Mauss as exemplifying two different critiques of religion.

Constance Furey

Constance Furey is Professor of Religious Studies at Indiana University Bloomington. A scholar of Renaissance and Reformation Christianity, she is the author of two monographs, *Erasmus, Contarini, and the Religious Republic of Letters* (2006), and *Poetic Relations: Intimacy and Faith in the English Reformation* (2017), and a forthcoming co-authored book, *Devotion: Three Inquiries in Religion, Literature, and the Political Imagination* (2021). She co-directs the "Being Human" project at Indiana University Bloomington, funded by the Luce Foundation, and convenes that project's Teaching Religion in Public forum.

W. Clark Gilpin

W. Clark Gilpin is the Margaret E. Burton Professor Emeritus at the University of Chicago Divinity School, where he served as dean from 1990 to 2000. From 2000 to 2004 he directed the Martin Marty Center, and he has also served as the director of the university's Nicholson Center for British Studies and as a member of the executive council of the university's Scherer Center for the Study of American Culture. Gilpin studies the history of modern Christianity, especially in relation to literature, and is currently writing about the letter from prison as a genre of religious literature in early modern England.

M. Cooper Harriss

M. Cooper Harriss is Associate Professor in the Department of Religious Studies at Indiana University Bloomington, where his teaching and research focus on American religion, literature, and culture. A co-editor of the journal *American Religion* and author of *Ralph Ellison's Invisible Theology* (2017), his work has appeared in *African American Review, The Journal of Africana Religions, Biblical Interpretation, The Journal of Religion,* and *Literature and Theology* (among other venues). His next project considers the boxer Muhammad Ali and the irony of American religion.

Elizabeth Shakman Hurd

Elizabeth Shakman Hurd is Professor of Political Science and Religious Studies and Crown Chair in Middle East Studies at Northwestern University. She is author of *The Politics of Secularism in International Relations* (2007) and *Beyond Religious Freedom: The New Global Politics of Religion* (2015), and co-editor of *Comparative Secularisms in a Global Age* (2010); *Politics of Religious Freedom* (2015), and *At Home and Abroad: The Politics of American Religion* (2021). She co-directed the "Politics of Religion at Home and Abroad" project and co-convenes, at Northwestern, the Global Religion and Politics Faculty Research Group.

Shaul Magid

Shaul Magid is Professor of Jewish Studies at Dartmouth College and Kogod Senior Research Fellow at the Shalom Hartman Institute of North America. His areas of interest and research include sixteenth century Kabbala, Hasidism, American Judaism, Jewish politics, and contemporary conceptions of Jewish religiosity. He is the author of numerous books including *From Metaphysics to Midrash: Myth, History, and the Interpretation of Scripture in Lurianic Kabbala* (2008) which was awarded the 2008 American Academy of Religion Award for best book in religion in the textual studies category, *Hasidism Incarnate* (2013), *The Bible the Talmud and the New Testament: Elijah Zvi Soloveitchik's Commentary to the Gospel* (2019), and *Meir Kahane: The Public Life and Political Thought of an American Jewish Radical* (2021).

Noah Salomon

Noah Salomon is Associate Professor of Religious Studies and the Irfan and Noreen Galaria Research Chair at the University of Virginia. From 2019–2021, Salomon was a Mellon New Directions Fellow circulating between Beirut, Muscat, and Khartoum, where he explored phenomena that sit at the intersection of Islam, the management of difference, and movements for popular sovereignty in the Middle East and Africa. He is author of *For Love of the Prophet: An Ethnography of Sudan's Islamic State*, winner of the 2017 Albert Hourani Prize from the Middle East Studies Association and an Excellence in the Study of Religion Book Award from the American Academy of Religion

Matthew Scherer

Matthew Scherer is Associate Professor of Government and Politics in the Schar School of Policy and Government at George Mason University. He directs the undergraduate program in Philosophy, Politics, and Economics, and teaches courses in ancient, modern, and contemporary political theory and constitutional law. He has held appointments as a Research Fellow at Georgetown University's Berkley Center for Religion, Peace, and World Affairs; as a Patrick Henry Postdoctoral Fellow at the Johns Hopkins University; and as an Andrew W. Mellon Postdoctoral Fellow in the Humanities at the University of California, Berkeley.

Lisa H. Sideris

Lisa Sideris is Professor of Environmental Studies at UC Santa Barbara. Her work focuses on the value and ethical significance of natural processes as these values are captured or occluded by religious and scientific worldviews. Her areas of research include environmental ethics, the environmental humanities, and the science-religion interface. She is particularly interested in the role of wonder in science, religion, and environmentalism and the ethics and implicit religiosity of emerging Anthropocene technologies like de-extinction and geoengineering. Her most recent book, *Consecrating Science: Wonder, Knowledge, and the Natural World* (2017) examines how scientific rhetoric and narratives about wonder actually pit science against religion and encourage a devaluation of the natural world.

Winnifred Fallers Sullivan

Winnifred Sullivan is Provost Professor in the Department of Religious Studies and Co-director of the Center of Religion and the Human at Indiana University Bloomington. She is author of *The Impossibility of Religious Freedom* (2005), *Prison Religion* (2009), A *Ministry of Presence* (2016), and *Church State Corporation* (2020) and co-editor of *Politics of Religious Freedom* (2016) and *At Home and Abroad* (2020).

Joseph Winters

Joseph Winters is Alexander F. Hehmeyer Associate Professor of Religious Studies and African and African American Studies at Duke University. His interests lie in African American religious thought, religion and critical theory, African-American literature, and Continental philosophy. Overall, his project is concerned with expanding conventional notions of black religiosity and black piety by drawing on resources from literature, philosophy, and critical theory. Winters' first book, *Hope Draped in Black: Race, Melancholy, and the Agony of Progress* (2016), examines how black literature and aesthetic practices challenge post-racial fantasies and triumphant accounts of freedom.